*The Dream of
Kilimanjaro*

The Dream of

of

Kilimanjaro

Rolf Edberg

Translated from the Swedish by
Keith Bradfield

Pantheon Books
New York

Library of Congress Cataloging in Publication Data

Edberg, Rolf, 1912–
    The dream of Kilimanjaro.

    Translation of *Dalens ande*.
    Bibliography: p.
    1. Human evolution. 2. Man. I. Title.
GN281.E313   1979   573.2   78-20415
ISBN 0-394-50384-8

To my daughter Birgitta
— pages from my diary of
a pilgrimage

The spirit of the valley can never die,
its name is the mysterious mother.

From the book of Tao

Contents

THOUGHTS UNDER AN UMBRELLA ACACIA

Thus Africa greets you,

with echoes from the earth's morning and the mystery of the as yet unrevealed, meditating on its past and expectant as to its future,

mighty in its age and strength, but still reflecting the unrest of creative geological forces, and fragile beneath the pressure of its growing human masses,

with abrupt contrasts and a bewildering diversity: the rich twilight of its dwindling rain forests alternating with the dazzling light of its expanding deserts; with a chill in the snowy mantles of Kilimanjaro and the Mountains of the Moon that can freeze the blood, while the stones in deep valleys sear like red-hot iron; mirroring itself in some of the world's largest lakes and rivers, and cowering under wild rainstorms, but at the same time the continent of constant droughts and thirsts; at once the richest and poorest of continents; overwhelming in its repose and devastating in its violence,

and yet, in all its sudden outward shifts and changes, resting in a sort in inward immutability,

in an eruption of colours, but with brown and green as the characteristic elements – brown, from the almost golden reflections of the savannahs during the dry period, from the deserts and parched river-beds to the heavy, livid tones of soils bleeding under the sharp hooves of cattle, and fires; green, playing in every conceivable shade from the forests, and seething in the grassland when they have been drenched by the rains – brown and green shimmering in the heat of noon, or subdued to soft pastel hues by the haze of dawn and dusk,

large enough to contain Europe, Arabia and India, with a myriad tribes and tongues, their skin pigment ranging from light copper to ebony, with the relics of pygmy peoples and men who in stature embody the giants of folk-tales; a meeting-place and a busy trail – for emigrants and for returning sons,

with a lingering multitude of creatures fancifully conjured forth by evolution, a lingering world of primaeval wildness and vitality, which shrinks a man, compelling him to throw his cloak of human self-sufficiency on the camp-fire,

and in all this: the pull towards a beginning, towards a *leit motif* that makes the past a matter of urgency. And brings it close.

Pilgrimage

I

When I fold the tent-door to the side, the dawn glows red as a camp-fire by the dark ridge of Lamagrut. I linger a while in the opening of the tent. Trying to capture the indeterminate instants in which the day begins to take shape. Noting how some acacias nearest the camp site free themselves from the darkness, how the landscape acquires firmer and firmer contours.

Dawn in the tropics is short. It unveils the landscape at observable speed, evoking its daytime appearance in a swiftly passing moment of time in which Nature seems to hold its breath.

The night wind has dropped. Its coolness lingers, but it will not be long before the heat of the day is trembling over savannah and plain. The thin grass appears golden and soft in the mild morning light: soon it will be dry and rough. A flock of gazelle which a moment ago stood delineated in ink against the red background of the dawn slip past not far from the tent, and melt into the grassland.

This landscape: so strong, so clean, so much at rest. Where it rises in a slow, sweeping swell to Naibor Soit, which with its primaeval rock and bushy vegetation stands up like an island from the sea of grass, everything is supremely self-evident.

Here is peace, and here are expanses over which a man

could wander for ever, without hurry and without purpose. I draw a few deep breaths, filling myself with a huge relief, a vital certainty. It's as if every cell were proclaiming, "This is where you belong".

My everyday self objects, refuses to listen. Even if I have experienced the same thing before when meeting Africa, I know how easy it is to confuse real moods with imagined. I have read and heard so much of other people's sense of coming home to this landscape that I have resolved to be keenly on my guard against any influences and preconceived sensations.

But as I try to tell myself the whole thing is imagination, I find the self-deception lies rather in my denial. The sense of having returned after a long while's absence is too strong to be disputed. It is something different from the feeling of *déja vu* that can sometimes seize one in an unfamiliar landscape. It is like a dream that refuses to be recalled, but which gnaws at the conscious mind with intimations as difficult to capture and retain as the shapes of an early dawn.

The years of toil, with happiness on those occasions you have felt whole, and dejection every time you recognized your "halfness", become remote and unimportant. It feels as if the reality was here, both a beginning and a fulfilment.

Something the cells remember. . . .

2

Nights filled with sounds, growing quiet towards morning –
sounds of hunting and flight, lust and fear. To lie under canvas
is to have them close.

The throaty, rasping growl of a lion from the ravine that
cuts through the high plain. Hammering hooves and shrill
neighs: kva-ha-ha, kva-ha-ha, zebras in flight. Between these
the yelping and howling of the hyenas, falling at times to
a moan of grief that seems to stem from the Dark Country
itself, or a grotesque giggle; rising on occasion to awful falsetto
blasts as the beast airs its satisfaction in killing or coupling.
The remote sirens of some jackals, the chatter and piping of a
flock of baboons that something has disturbed, heavy wingbeats
as the vultures lift from their treetops just before dawn to start
their all-seeing reconnaissance of the savannah. All recorded
and syncopated by the night wind that blows through thorn and
grass, and tugs at the tent-pegs.

Sounds that the darkness magnifies and makes more distinct.
Sounds of events that are near, but that can still only be
surmised.

So different from the night sounds of a Nordic forest.
And yet strangely unalien. The voices of the tropical night
awake, surprisingly, a remote response within yourself. A

response of fear and attraction, wonder and certainty.

Moving about the savannah by day, you feel painfully like an intruder in a world belonging to other creatures, keenly observed on all sides. You must be still, find the rhythm and enter it in order to be accepted as part of the pattern – a pattern that is at once relaxation and taut readiness to act.

Suddenly you see the gnu and the Grant's gazelle start and stiffen into statues. It may be an unintentional movement on your part. Or some other cause you fail to comprehend. A movement, perhaps, in the grass. Perhaps the warning flight of some birds. The creatures of the grassland are linked to each other in an efficient warning system: the sharp hearing of one species, the sight of another, the nose of a third complement each other, so that the one can deduce from the others' reactions whether or not danger threatens. You yourself perceive only the sudden, almost unreal stillness, until it is resolved in flight or relaxation.

Many herbivores also seem to possess an almost mystical ability to interpret the intentions of carnivores. The impala, stitching the ground with playful leaps, seems to know whether or not the wild dogs, those gnomes that emerge wraithlike from their holes in the ground, are actually on the hunt – if so, it flees, otherwise it continues to graze unconcerned in the predator's vicinity.

Early man, who lived on the same terms as the other beasts of the earth, must in the same way have known intuitively or by experience whether or not he had anything to fear. His life among the other species was a co-existence in which not the fear but surely the watchfulness could be permanent. As a rule, man was probably not greatly threatened – his scent was un-attractive, the taste of his flesh inferior. But as he himself hunted, so he too could still be the prey, above all at times when better food was wanting. Therefore, he had to be able to conclude from the look and movement of an animal, the expelled breath of a lion, the sudden call of a bird, the flapping sail of an elephant's ear, whether or not danger was at hand.

He had to be able to interpret the sights of day, and the sounds of night.

It is, surely, the recollection of a fear once associated with specific situations that can flare up in many Africans who have only recently left the wilds behind them. But the counter-pole of fear is also there: a sense of secret understanding.

Something of all this is awakened in you as you listen to the sounds of the tropical night. Something within you has always wanted to return to the darkness. Another darkness – or perhaps just this darkness.

3

Can the cells remember? The cells in our skin and muscles, in the blood and nerve-endings, irises and ear-drums? Remember over hundreds of thousands, millions, of years?

Conventional wisdom would have denied this: the storehouse of memory is built into the brain, and can only store your individual impressions and experiences – they are kept there, safely locked away, all that you have seen and heard and been present at, every second of your life.

But as you sit there in the opening of a tent, the sounds of night lingering within you and a morning country with a blue sun-haze on the horizon in front of you, you realize with un-reasoning clarity that this answer will not do. You feel the savannah winds of the ages sweeping through your soul, and experience how your cells and senses are ready to accept this landscape with its lines and sounds because they know the wavelength.

What do we know? In the space of a few years much con-ventional wisdom has been overthrown, much that was self-evident dissolved in uncertainty.

A contemporary depth psychology allows us to hazard a collective unconscious which deep under the many layers of the conscious binds us to all our fellow-travellers in the present and with the humans and near-humans who trod the paths of the past. Perhaps ultimately, there exists some sort of sounding-board, or medium of resonance, common to everything in Creation; in the dark depths, capillaries may surely persist through which in past ages flowed lights and sounds from these East African savannahs that hide the key to what we subsequently became. Recent observations have shown that the amoebae, those microscopic lumps of protoplasm, seem to possess some sort of memory. This excites a fancy that our individual cells may be capable of storing memory-impulses. What we now think we can glimpse of the strange ways of evolution hardly precludes the possibility of such impulses being carried further from generation to generation.

The sensual ties existing between Nature as a generally intelligible totality and one's ultimate ''I'' must somewhere have an anchorage. Why should not previous generations' perceptions of smells and sounds and moods exist as vague memory-traces, perhaps in the DNA molecules, the bearers of our genetic heritage – persisting there as a memory belonging to the species itself, beneath the matter that is registered by and vanishes with the individual?

The hypnotic mood prevailing in the East African landscape invites a layman to toy with this thought, that somewhere in the cell nuclei there may be a sort of non-oblivion that can be activated in a specific situation or surroundings. That the sensation of returning may be due to some chemical cell-reaction which is in accord with something in just this environment.

4

This is a pilgrimage. That is how we planned it, my wife and I. When our black friends Inzoka and Ndambuka and Wambua, and white Patrick, packed our landcruisers with tents and water containers and other gear for a long trek, and we left the regular roads, it was because we wanted to capture the mood of the valley in which man as a species seems to have been begotten.

This is why we raise our tent and light our fire on these yellow savannahs, by some water-hole in the desert, or occasionally in the luxury of a rain forest.

One can say, perhaps, that we are seeking the "spirit" of the valley, although we have hesitated to put it so openly. Yet it brushes against us continually, as we move from camp-site to camp-site. It is there in our unreasoning sense of being close to something we have vaguely sought. It suspends the past tense of what has gone, letting it slip instead into an extended now.

Nothing hacks time to pieces. The days are joined one to the other, but how they may be cut up into hours and seconds or bundled together in weeks is a matter of indifference. The only thing that gives our time a measure is the waxing and waning of the moon, or the indefinable mood of expectancy when the thirsty soil senses that rain cannot be far away. But all this has the rhythm of repetition.

In such a rhythm, distances backwards in time also cease to have any meaning. You would not find it in the least remarkable if some low-browed near-humans emerged from the shadows of the valley, and hunked down by your camp-fire.

The basic plan of this landscape cannot have altered much in the last two million years. Now as then, Lamagrut raises its mute volcanic cone over the plain; the same dawn fires burn by its ridge. And wandering through the rough grass up towards Naibor Soit, you felt you were following in the tracks of some other who had had business there.

Olduvai. Below the camp-site is the cleft in which the remains of near-humans and early humans, after a long night in beds of sediment, recently re-encountered the African sun. This is the point to which a pilgrimage in the Valley must initially lead.

Farther away, however, preparations are glimpsed which began under other climes. The road to the Valley went via Gondwanaland.

5

Gondwanaland – the name lies like a poem on the tongue, it quickens the imagination. Gondwanaland was one of our beginnings.

Throughout the Seventies, we have been on a journey of discovery as exciting as any of those voyages that once linked the continents together over the oceans. We are in process of exploring the earth in a new dimension. New knowledge is being acquired, old knowledge reinterpreted. An overall picture is taking shape that lends context to much which has previously seemed random and capricious.

The continents, on which we mill around and make world history, no longer stand out as firm rocks, solidly anchored in the earth's interior. Instead we see the outer shell of the earth as being divided into a number of plates, which are drifting around like floats on the globe's viscous substratum, and constantly changing their position and shape. The real history of the world is that of drifting continental floes.

The theory of continents that had hung together and then drifted apart emerged naturally and at an early stage when it was noticed how the Atlantic coasts of America and Europe-Africa fitted each other. Today we can find the evidence with the help of sophisticated instruments, and read the details in the earth's own writing as it is inscribed in ancient volcanic matter and in sediment on the ocean beds.

The material from volcanic eruptions that occurred hundreds and millions of years ago contains, frozen inside, a magnetism that reveals the orientation of the earth's magnetic field at the time. This sort of fossilized magnetism from a given geological era can point in different directions on different continents. Since it is impossible that widely disparate magnetic poles could have existed contemporaneously, the continents must have been in different positions from now.

A comparative script is available in the meteoric dust that in the form of magnetic particles of nickel, iron, cobalt and copper is constantly streaming in from the cosmos, and floating down to the earth's surface in snowflakes and raindrops. Slowly this matter sinks through the oceans, silts up on the sea-bed, and there arranges itself in a pattern directed towards the magnetic pole. As the millions of years pass, layer upon layer of such particles accumulate. By reading the changing direction of these cosmic compass-needles, it is possible to see how the poles changed places, and how the continents drifted. By collating these data from the earth's own register and putting computers to work on them one can obtain a picture of the globe at different eras of time.

Two hundred million years ago, when the first dinosaurs began to heave their armoured bodies over the land, the earth's present continents were conjoined in a single supercontinent, which geologists have dubbed *Pangaea*. It groped out over the globe with two giant arms. The northern arm, *Laurasia*, comprised what is now North America, Europe and Asia. The southern arm, *Gondwanaland*, stretching down over the present Antarctic, comprised what is now South America, Australia, India and Africa. Between the two arms of this continent lay a primaeval ocean, the *Sea of Tethys*.

Then the great continent began to break up. A rift valley opened up in a north-south direction. The event was accompanied by violent volcanic explosions, the erupted matter from which helps us to determine the date. Slowly by human concepts of time, but inexorably on the geological time-scale, the rift filled with water and broadened into the Atlantic that now separates Africa from South America, and Eurasia from North America.

New rifts appeared. Australia was torn loose from Gondwanaland. and sailed towards its present location. Another fragment, which was to be the Indian subcontinent, drifted up over the Sea of Tethys and fifty million years ago encountered the great Eurasian floe in a collision that is still taking place, imperceptibly to human observation but violently in the geological perspective. Where the collision occurred, the edge of the one floe was raised up over the other, as when ice-floes clash during a spring storm. Part of the sea-bed by the colliding coasts buckled and rose up in the sky – which explains why one finds high up on the northern slopes of the Himalayas thick layers of shells from marine creatures that lived in the ocean one hundred and fifty million years ago.

The major part of Gondwanaland, which was to comprise Africa with Arabia and some of the Mediterranean peninsulae, drifted towards Eurasia in similar manner: the earth's newly discovered writing allows us to follow its journey over the Sea of Tethys, while the rifling of ice beneath the Sahara indicates its starting-point: near the South Pole. When the continents met, Arabia was torn loose from the African plate and helped in wrinkling up the mountains of Iran, while Italy, Jugoslavia and Greece drifted towards Europe, where they were pressed into the continent, and helped fold the Alps and the Carpathians. As if modelled in soft wax, there was created along the original southern coast of Europe a practically coherent chain of mountains composed of material from the edges of the drifting floes, and from the bed of the primaeval ocean.

Everywhere, the land surface bears the traces of what happened and is happening at this moment where the continental floes are separating from each other along deep ocean ridges and pressing against each other in the areas of collision.

Volcanic eruptions and earthquakes are self-evident phenomena along these unquiet lines.

Nor have living things, the plants and animals, been untouched, as the passengers of these floes. The drifting of the continents has determined in very high degree the conditions of life and the course of evolution on this planet.

The radiation where volcanic cauldrons have boiled over; the volcanic ash that has silted up on slopes and plains; the mountains that have been raised, and the valleys that have been hollowed out where the water flushed down the slopes, carrying pulverised rock; climatic changes depending on where the floes drifted, and what heights and depths they helped create – all these things affected life and its forms in a continuous interplay between geological forces and natural organisms.Written in your own bones and tissues are the half-expunged signatures of the life-forms to which this interplay once gave birth.

We are also beginning to decode the address of our more remote home. The new geology is creating large, as yet hardly explored, opportunities to follow the development of life on Earth. It seems that Gondwanaland functioned from the beginning as a coherent "evolutionary area", in only sporadic contact with Laurasia. It has been demonstrated that a number of primitive life-forms such as dragonflies and midges are of exclusively Gondwanian origin.

As Africa slowly drifted over the Sea of Tethys, a primate also began to develop in the green twilight of its forests, a primate from whose loins were to issue monkeys and baboons, chimpanzees and humankind. As yet his genes carried only possibilities, the realization of which presupposed certain external forces.

One of his descendants would one day, for his own purposes, attempt further to manipulate what had been produced in the earth's crust by the preceding play of geological forces. The mineral finds that appear to be the result of pressing, bending and heating when the drifting floes clashed, these he would grind to pieces and transform into spears and picks, dinosaurian tanks and space-ships. The coal, oil and limestone formed by

17

organic life that had never been allowed to decay in the normal way, he would put to use – the coal and oil to liberate a fossilized energy which came to characterize his entire way of life, the limestone from fossilized marine creatures to raise pyramids and cathedrals.

The play of geological forces produced in other words a creature who himself became a geological force.

Man was a biological consequence of the continental drift, a creature of the Gondwanian line.

Nor is the journey at an end. Everything is in an "ongoing" state, in which no part of the earth has come to rest, no form of life is definitive. Our current names for rivers and coasts, continents and oceans are dated and temporary – as are the specific names we give to different expressions of life. The continents continue to move – admittedly only at the rate of a couple of centimetres per year, but this still means two thousand kilometres per hundred million years. Africa and Europe will be pressed closer to each other, until the Mediterranean disappears and its bed is raised to form a new chain of mountains. The Atlantic will continue to expand while the Pacific shrinks, until Eurasia and America meet again on the opposite side to that where they separated a hundred and fifty million years ago.

And while new shores rise from new oceans, and new ranges of mountains rise against new horizons, the forms of life will be relentlessly refashioned – as long as life on Earth persists.

6

Like a couple of termites on the move, our landcruisers seek their way through the huge trough that is the Great Rift Valley. East and west of us, steep blue-black walls of rock rise up five, six, seven hundred metres to the high plateau. As far as the eye can see, they seem to run in straight, parallel lines some thirty miles apart.

Since the geologists began tapping at these walls with their tiny hammers in the late nineteenth century, various theories have been aired as to the genesis of the Valley. In the light of the new geology, it emerged – like the Atlantic and the Himalayas – as the work of the same forces as set the continental floes in motion.

Rock datings suggest that the first crack began to form when Africa was still part of Gondwanaland. The unrest of the earth's crust continued during the voyage over the Sea of Tethys. The decisive events apparently began twenty million years ago, when Africa collided with Eurasia. Contemporaneously with the ruptures in the African floe that wrenched Arabia and Madagascar loose and drove Italy like a shaft into the underbelly of Europe, the earth also in this area – weak already from previous ruptures – was stretched and prized open.

Finally, a long strip of earth running straight across the East African plateau dropped to a depth of a thousand metres. The rift spread to the north and south, producing a crevasse that extended for one sixth of the earth's circumference, from the Taurus Mountains in Turkey, in the north, to the coastline of Mozambique fronting the Indian Ocean in the south. In its six-thousand-mile course, the crevasse creates room for the River Jordan and the Sea of Galilee and for the Dead and the Red Seas with offshoots towards Suez and the Gulf of Aden, to reach the present continent of Africa in the infernoes of the Dana depression and the Afar Valley with temperatures of over 70 degrees Centigrade in the shade, areas where today odd remnants of humanity that have adapted to their hostile sur-roundings watch over their scant resources of water with bloodthirsty eyes, their castrating knives at the ready. Having cleft the Ethiopian mountains, the mainline of the crevasse embarks, at Lake Turkana (formerly Rudolf), on its course through Kenya and Tanzania, while a subsidiary traverses Uganda in an arc – creating the space for a series of lakes, which were linked together until the Mountains of the Moon rose to separate them – and plunges into Lake Tanganyika with a water level eight hundred metres over the ocean and a bed seven hundred metres below the sea level before rejoining the main crevasse at the beginning of Lake Malawi. Where the continent was broken asunder, lakes were upended and the outlets of some were sealed off, while new outlets opened up for others.

The force that prized up this crack in the fabric of the earth has continued to act in the last few million years: some of man's hominoid predecessors must have watched its effects with wonder and terror. Along the line of the rift, the earth's glowing interior bubbled, hissed and roared up through hundreds of volcanoes. The earth bled. The volcanoes that were to form Kilimanjaro and Mount Kenya were lifted more than five thousand metres skywards: today they rise directly out of the plain, with no intermediary mountain chains, contributing as much as the deep valley itself to the special character of East Africa.

Mild earthquakes, boiling hot springs and some thirty active or semi-active volcanoes inform us that the forces which created the Rift Valley are still active. Just as the Red Sea and the Gulf of Aden are still gradually being forced open by continental drift, so can the stretching processes along the Valley continue until new breaking-points are reached. By some time in another twenty million years or so the eastern half of the area that today forms Ethiopia, Kenya and Tanzania may have broken loose and drifted out to sea to form an island the size of Madagascar, while the Valley, along whose bed we crawl termitelike, has become an arm of the sea.

7

We pitch camp at Losiolo on top of the eastern wall of the Valley, at about the height of Sweden's Mount Kebnekajse. The nights strike cool after the throbbing heat of the Valley, and the night wind blows at times so hard that we are forced to tether our tent with heavy lines to one of the landcruisers. The flames from our fire jet out horizontally over the abyss.

We had expected to be alone up here. By day, however, we have the company of a Samburu family, for whom our camp is obviously an event. The materfamilias is a tall, stately woman with a profile of classical purity and a dazzling white smile. She arrives with bow and quiver, a black Diana, bare-bosomed like her many daughters of different vintages. They settle down in the shade of a tree, lean their water gourds against its trunk, and study our doings in silence. A couple of young Samburu warriors with tight plaits smeared with red ochre remain more withdrawn, pretending not to watch us, and finally seat themselves a little way down the slope, so that all we see is their broad-bladed spears sticking up over the edge of the rift.

The view out over the Valley is strikingly beautiful. Just in front of our tent the eastern rift wall drops with dizzying abruptness, while the western wall is glimpsed as a misty blue backcloth on the other side. Immediately below us lies an area of low, wildly sculptured rocks, which give way to the flat, yellow floor of the Valley, also clad in light bluish mist. Right now I am hardly aware of the fact that the seemingly solid rock beneath my feet is slowly moving, and that this prospect and whole panorama are no more than passing. Our eyes are automatically drawn to the floor of the Valley. No life is apparent down there, neither men nor beasts, but the Samburu tell us of leopards and buffaloes living on the valley-bed. A number of paths like thin yellow strips can be seen twisting and turning below, interspersed with small white flecks, the ashes of dead camp-fires.

I strain my eyes in search of other camp-fires, long since extinguished, seeking also a life that seethed when the only fires burning were those lit in the grassland and bush by lava and volcanic ash.

Perhaps ultimately it was precisely such a fire, volcanic rather than kindled by lightning, subterranean rather than celestial, that a two-legged creature used to make his first camp-fire, thus altering the entire terms and conditions of his species.

If so, it was surely consistent. Volcanic fire had previously changed the conditions of life in more than one respect, and may have directly affected the course of evolution itself. In the very beginning, volcanic activity may have helped breathe life into the matter of this planet. The water in clouds and oceans, the nitrogen in the air, the carbon whose unstable atom gives life its backbone – all these may have their origins in eruptions from the underworld.

The great thrusts and spasms of the geological process, the vast ejaculations from the interior of the earth, must have had a decisive effect on the evolution of life in the Valley and its immediate vicinity. We encounter traces of volcanic activity everywhere. In the coniform rocks and mountains; in bare landscapes where the blocks of lava produced by comparatively recent eruptions lie so tightly packed that only occasional rough grass and a few thorn-bushes find space between them. Above

23

all we find such traces on the savannahs and grasslands, on which the monsoons have scattered ash from the volcanoes in the highlands, and rained it down to form layers of fertile, water-retaining mould. These showers of volcanic ash, and erosion from the edges of the highlands, have raised the bed of the Valley several hundred metres above its original level.

In the past, this land must have furnished the ecological basis of a vast body of wildlife – enormous in its number, diversity and individual life-mass. In spite of mass slaughter in recent years, the world's richest wild fauna is still to be found in the Valley and its vicinity. Here, too, runs one of the major migratory routes of countless European birds. Sodium, washed from volcanic dust down into undrained lakes on the valley-bed, gives rise to a distinctive and unusual form of animal life. Poisonous to mammals, this bitter concoction provides, in combination with the shimmering heat, a wonderful environment for Diatomas and other algae, which propagate at enormous speed, dye the lakes red as wine or pink as candy, and furnish the nutritional basis for the world's most spectacular ornithological display, the millions of flamingoes that turn the lakes into pools of fire.

When the earth split under the pressure from within, radio-activity also flowed out. This may have caused mutations, which would explain the lavish variety of life-forms that so quickly succeeded each other. Only a few species survived the cataclysms unchanged – including the crocodiles, which present as they slide into Lake Turkana or Lake Baringo at your approach roughly the same appearance as they would have done a hundred and thirty million years ago. But the bulk of the larger animals living only two or three million years ago have vanished, leaving descendants whose shape and appearance are in certain respects wholly different.

While the ice-caps drew back and forth over the northern hemisphere and periods of rain and drought, cool weather and feverish climates succeeded each other in the tropics, and the radioactivity poured out from the bared interior of the earth, the alchemy of the elements was at work also on the primates. Varying sorts of man-ape and ape-man were fashioned, some of them soon to disappear, others to evolve further.

One of these experiments produced man. That so many relics of pre-humans, near-humans, and early-humans have been found just in East Africa cannot be due simply to the fact that the tufa and rich sedimentation created unusually good repositories for fossils. All the evidence that we can now interpret suggests that the part of ancient Gondwanaland where evolution experimented with so many varieties of primate was also man's own birthplace. It might be that the radioactivity brought about the mutation which proved so fateful for this planet.

The great crevasse in the high tropical plateau became the very vagina of the earth whose labour brought forth from dusky depths our own race.

8

So to Olduvai.

To the east, a misty blue cone that the Massai call Oldoinyo Lengai or "The Mountain of God". The god enthroned on its heights, like the god another migrant people saw on Sinai, must have a certain weakness for violent natural phenomena. Oldoinyo Lengai is a vigorous young volcano which as recently as in 1966 in a fit of extravagant energy flung out lava that transformed its previously grass-brown slopes into a tropical snowscape, as contact with the air turned it into glittering white sodium carbonate.

But Lamagrut has aged, reposing now in silent dignity on the plain. Only a couple of million years ago it too belched glowing boulders and ash over the surrounding country. It rolled out a floor of lava, on which layer after layer of sediment has subsequently been laid, red layers alternating with grey, and brown with blue, so that the soil, in cross-section, looks like a rainbow cake.

Just beyond our camp site, there lay in the remote past a long, narrow lake fringed with bowstring hemp which is known to the Massai as olduvai and has given the place its name. As the layers of sediment increased, the shoreline altered and the lake was corseted off into a number of smaller lakes. Through this depression a watercourse incised its way, in comparatively recent times, ever deeper into the hundred-metre-thick layers of sediment until it reached the lava-studded bed. A winding canyon was formed, on the slopes of which the green arrows of olduvai hemp still shoot upwards.

Where the river hacked down through the sediment, the vertebrae, limbs and crania of a vanished wildlife were washed clean. The German lepidopterist Kattwinkel, searching for rare species of insects shortly before the Great War, happened by accident on the ravine and found himself in one of the largest charnel-houses in the world. The relics of three-toed horses, of elephants with their tusks turned down like walruses, of hippopotamuses with eyes on periscopes moving over the surface of the water, of short-necked, great-horned giraffes, and sheep as large as buffaloes, stuck out from the layers of sand. His discovery caused a brief sensation, which was soon overshadowed by the news from the front.

In the early Thirties the palaeontologist and archaeologist Louis Leakey, the son of a couple of English missionaries and himself born in a leaf hut in the mountains of the Kikuyu, began with his wife Mary to take an interest in the ravine and its fossils. Nor were the Leakeys content simply to search for the remains of extinct and previously unknown animal species. Their working hypothesis was that where so many animals had foregathered, it should also be possible to find the predecessors of man himself.

In 1959, when the first satellites had already carried man into the Space Age, there started a series of discoveries in the field of human pre-history, discoveries that were to make Leakey the best-known and most controversial name in contemporary archaeology, and Olduvai Gorge the Mecca of evolutionists the world over. It was Mary Leakey who discovered in the former river-bed a skull with a raked forehead, heavy superciliary arches, and a powerful jaw. The new process of radioactive dating established its age at the astonishing figure of almost two million years. The name originally given to this resurrected creature was *Zinjanthropus*, East African man. After further finds had been made, which revealed the parallel existence of a heavy limbed and a more slender hominid, the two varieties were classified, together with Dart's finds from South Africa, under the blanket name of *Australopithecus*.

Even these finds excited attention, enthusiasm, and doubt.

They were followed by a rapid succession of more advanced finds, which Leakey dubbed *Homo habilis*, or "handy" man, owing to his skill in making stone tools, and an African version of *Homo erectus*, or "upright" man, who is spread over Asia and Europe and is regarded as the most immediate ancestor of *Homo sapiens*. At the greatest remote we glimpse *Ramapithecus*, whom Leakey discovered in a stony orange grove in the Victoria basin, and whose genes were to be carried forward through fourteen million years to a species that would one day take off into space.

The very diversity of the finds puts Olduvai in a class of its own. But the main result of "forty years of crawling up and down the slopes with your eyes only a few inches from the ground", to use Leakey's words, was a radical extension of the time scale of human evolution. Olduvai broadened man's horizon backwards in time, Olduvai is also unique in that it seems to have been continuously inhabited ever since the first hominid pitched his camp by the lakeside to our own day, when the Massai build their manyattas along the edge of the ravine. Olduvai shows us evolution at work: from *Australopithecus* in the lowest stratum to *Homo erectus* in the surface sediment, the different finds are ranged in apparently ordered sequence, with the brains increasing in volume and increasingly human features.

Olduvai also allows us to follow the way in which the hominid's hands become increasingly skilled as he struggled to extend his territory: from rough chips of stone to more and more finely-worked hand-wedges as the different cultures were stacked one on the other. One can follow these creatures on journeys made specifically in order to bring back to their settlements the types of stone best suited for fashioning tools.

For a long time their favourite stone was the hard, flinty volcanic obsidian that could be obtained from Lamagrut – the tribute paid by the underworld to tool-making man.

It is impossible to discern the more distinct features of these various creatures: even so, they become remarkably alive as they leave their resting-places in the sediment to re-encounter the African sun.

We see them as they interact with the environment. The terrain tells us how the climate has shifted, affecting the conditions of life. It gives us a glimpse of what the water and the savannah meant as a life-path for the evolving hominid. We see the hominids as they interact with other species, now largely extinct. At least in part, we can follow their diet: from mice, lizards, snakes, birds and the smaller fish to the larger beasts of prey. We can, apparently, trace their seasonal migrations, as they followed the nomadic creatures of the grasslands, only to return generation after generation to the olduvai-fringed lake – gatherers and hunters, exploiting the nutritional openings afforded by the different seasons. And we guess that at times they squatted by the shore, staring fearfully as the sky burned over the craters to the east.

Louis Leakey died a few years ago, revered and accorded a status equal almost to that of Darwin by the scientific societies which initially doubted his theories and conclusions. Mary Leakey lives on in a simple cottage by the brink of the famous ravine, surrounded by her own and her husband's work, her nearest neighbours a few Massai. Agile as a mountain goat, she shows us round the sites of the various finds – a grand old lady of archaeology, active, full of vitality, content at the close of an exciting life, and still engaged in new enterprises.

Mary and Louis Leakey would have liked to believe that some branch of the Australopithecenes they had unearthed, as well as *Homo habilis*, constituted a natural link in the chain from *Ramapithecus* to our own species. They fitted so neatly into the Olduvai pattern of development.

But something and someone was to upset the picture.

9

1470. A number in a catalogue. And yet what does it not contain of evolution – and revolution?

One feels this palpably, almost like something brushing the skin, as one sits in the spartan work-room of Richard Leakey, who has succeeded his father as head of Kenya's National Museum. He has also followed his parents' lead in the search for man's ancestors. He and his wife Meave constitute the new Leakey research team, seeking paths back to man's origins with the same fervour as the earlier couple.

His childhood in Olduvai gave him the fossil-hunter's trained eye for where in a given terrain it can be worth searching. When, as the co-ordinator of an international dig by the River Omo in Ethiopia, he flew on repeated occasions over the browny grey wastes of Northern Kenya, where the untrained eye sees only deserts and semi-deserts, he was nagged, increasingly, by the conviction that there, somewhere, lay the solution.

Shortly afterwards, when he began his search on the ground – initially with the help of camels hired from a desert tribe, the Gabbra – the desert kept its word. His first find was made while strolling round a camp he had had to improvise because one of the camels, after a strenuous march, refused point blank to continue in the wild terrain. High on a sand dune, beside a thorn bush, he suddenly saw staring at him an almost complete cranium with heavy superciliary arches and raked forehead, obviously uncovered only a few months previously by the shifting sand: an *Australopithecus*, encountered practically on the tenth anniversary of his mother's famous find – and six hundred thousand years older. As testimony that near-man had developed hardly at all over a good half million years it provided an interesting hint, although as yet no solution.

The great find was to come a couple of years later, when they found in a greyish-brown slope near a deep gulley over one hundred and fifty fragments of skull, some of them no larger than a thumbnail, which Meave Leakey succeeded in laboriously piecing together. There emerged a handsome, long cranium: no ape-like superciliary arches, but what was almost a vaulted forehead, the least human aspect being the flat nasal section. In view of the wide variants which are found in the human race, the skull, as far as its shape was concerned, could well have been that of a living human being. Calcium-argon dating of the tuff layers between which it was found points to an age of 2–2.5 million years.

Nameless, lacking any designation of species, the skull hides in the museum's collection of fossils under the neutral-sounding catalogue number 1470. But it is a find that has further extended our horizon backwards in time. With 1470, mankind has penetrated nearly a million years closer to its origins, although along a different path from that which it had previously sought. While the later near-human *Australopithecus* from Olduvai had a brain volume of 530 cu.cm. and the even later *Homo habilis* 630–680 cu.cm., 1470 has a brain volume of 810 cu.cm., as compared with our own figure of 1,400 cu.cm. It shatters the previous pattern, according to which the fossils found could be neatly ordered in evolving sequences. The low-browed *Australopithecus* is no longer a possible ancestor of man, but represents a lateral line, a marked and inhibited cousin who met his end in one of evolution's blind alleys. So far as we can tell today, it is in 1470 that we see our own image.

I sit with Richard Leakey, 1470 in my hand, letting my fingers pass cautiously over the lines of the skull, looking into a cavity that once contained a small human brain.

I seek some kind of contact with the silent face in front of me, trying to obtain a flesh-and-blood impression of the creature who once journeyed and rested, fought for his life, and propagated his species in the valley where man was born.

High up in the Valley, in a sun-drenched wasteland by a jade-green sea, stands Koobi Fora, the base camp for Richard Leakey's field studies.

It had to be included in our pilgrimage. We filled water-containers and petrol cans to the brim, and managed to get up a sports plane laden with fresh food before starting the laborious crawl through a desert in which we could be reduced to what we could carry with us. The entire eastern shore of this jade-green sea is uninhabited except for a tiny vestige of humanity, the El molo tribe at Loiyangalani, furthest to the south. Northward the desert spills its lava right up towards the Sudan and Ethiopia. Previously Shifta warriors from Somalia used to raid the area, for a while forcing the El molo to live on an island out in the lake, to avoid total extinction; ten years ago, they killed the two whites then living in Loiyangalani. Now, the Shifta warriors have been quiescent for some years. Apart from the bone-hunting team in Koobi Fora, the chances of encountering anyone in this area are slight.

We live in a hut, mortared in rough stone to breast height, with a rush roof above and open in between to the wind, which at nights blows pleasantly cool. We hear at night the clatter of small crocodiles down by the shore. By day, they cautiously withdraw when we go down to cool off in the water, which is made brackish by volcanic salts. Further out, the water seethes with larger crocodiles, whose good fortune it is to be left in peace by man since their salt-pickled skin is not appreciated in ladies' shoes and hand-bags. On the shore, salty spike-grass.

When Count Teleki von Szék, a Hungarian, arrived on the southern shore of the jade-green sea in the late Eighties, with four hundred and fifty bearers, six guides, and a collection of interpreters into different tribal languages, he believed in white man's fashion that he had discovered it, and in his white man's way he gave it a name, calling it, by coincidence, after the dual monarchy's Crown Prince Rudolf, who by now would surely be entirely forgotten were it not for the echo of the Meyerling drama. Others, although of darker pigment, had seen the lake before. They had also named it: *Basso Narok*. Or, among the Gabbra people, *Galani Boi,* which they say means Great Water.

A fitting name for a lake that can be whipped into a lather, and to roaring waves, when the wind gets up, and which in size is outstripped by only twenty-two lakes in the entire world. But not even those who originally gave the lake its name were its discoverers. 1470 had lived by its shores when its surface was seventy metres higher then the present level, and footprints in the sands of time may indicate that even his ancestors evolved by the shores of the Great Water, or the Even Greater Water.

Modern archaeology is teamwork – however much its driving force may be favoured by an interplay between coincidence and the trained eye of the observer. Up here in what is perhaps the largest fossil-bearing area in the world, archaeology and palaeontology work hand in hand with biology and meteorology in the best organized investigation into our past that has yet been launched. A key person in the team is the geologist. He provides the map the fossil-hunters use to orient themselves in bygone landscapes.

A few days spent with the expedition's geologist, who in four years has charted the landscape as it has shifted over the last four million years, bring to life what the eye otherwise experiences as barren. We gnaw our way slowly forward by jeep through a terrain shaped by water, winds and volcanoes. First over the old lake-bed, where dwarf acacias and thorn trees provide food for a few gerenuk antelopes, and where oryxes have drawn a fine shuntyard of trails in the sand. Then up towards the desert areas with their shimmering mirages and a heat that presses down like a weight over the landscape. There is fever in the air, lashing us like the blows of a whip.

When my mentor shows me the clearly marked spirals in the sand strata, indicating where the Great Water met the shore at different periods in time, the landscape alters. The depressions are filled with water, and new shores are clad in verdant green. I find myself journeying simultaneously in two landscapes: the present wasteland and a past Eden, sprung from the lava beds of a still more remote past.

A sand dune in the wasteland, to the untrained eye a detail in the monotonous grey-brown scene, suddenly becomes genuinely interesting. A few years ago a number of hewn stone chips were found, some of them sharp, others worn by constant use. Calcium-argon dating put the age of these primitive tools close to 2 million years. We are standing on the site of one of the oldest-known human settlements, and one of the oldest-known manufactories of tools, older than corresponding finds in Olduvai.

The desert ceases to be desert. The sand dune becomes a populated shore, shadowed by spreading trees: below runs a river of crystal, widening out into a small lake. It is brought home to one that the beginnings of culture had to occur where there was water to drink – water was not something that could be transported, it had to be sought out. A few antelope and crocodile teeth which we find together with some hewn stone chips confirm in their way that this was a place where land and water met. It also provides a hint as to the company man kept around 2 million years ago.

A few hours later we halt the jeep by another desert ledge, clamber down the side of a valley, and work our way up the opposite slope. There stands a simple greyish-white pole with a number: 1470. Our pilgrimage is at an end.

I sit here a while in silence, and experience again how the scene changes. Through the valley we have just struggled across there flows a river, from which hippopotami rise snorting. The jaw of such an animal with well-preserved teeth, and contemporary with 1470, juts out of the gravel to give life to the picture. On the other side of the ledge is a lush fenland, the nearest ridges verdant with growth. Beyond them the Even Greater Water, nourished by tropical streams and not yet brackish: the sound reaches us of waves lapping against the shore.

There can have been no settlement here: the ridge between the river and the fenland is too narrow. Something else must have brought 1470 to his last resting-place – possibly the search for food, perhaps the curiosity that became the badge of his species.

You seem to be weighing, again, a cranium in your hands, tracing its lines with your fingertips, groping for some sort of answer. What can you expect to find? Even your own generation consists mostly of averted faces. How then, tied as you are to the assumptions and concepts of your own day, could you ever hope to meet and make contact with someone beyond the forests and deserts of time? You can see the shapes passably enough: femurs that have escaped the bone-breaking jaws of the hyenas (which have otherwise rendered such finds rare from the days before man buried his dead) suggest a body height of about 160 cm. – as in the living fossils of our own day, the pygmies of the rain forests and the bushmen of the Kalahari Desert. You can catch glimpses of how he lived. But nothing betrays the slightest hint as to the curve of the mouth, the colour of the hair, the smell of the skin – and still less what once went on between the frontal lobes.

And yet there is something there which with self-evident simplicity merges into that elusive sense of having returned.

35

10

Wilds and space. There is something symbolic in the fact that with our "eyes only a few inches from the ground" we have etched our way deeper and deeper into our own past, and begun at the same time to see our planet in full perspective from outside. The same hand that shaped the first rough tools of stone now handles the instrument panels in space ships.

Most writers of history portray technological and cultural development as a series of leaps and suddennesses. There, in the great arc of fertile river valleys in the Middle East we suddenly find agricultural man, with the skill to cultivate cereal grasses that gave civilization its economic base. There, the Egyptians and Babylonians emerge with an advanced mathematics based on the unit of twelve, with funds of astronomical knowledge, and with written characters that gave language its second birth. There, the intellectual adventures of the Hellenes began.

But nothing of all this can have occurred suddenly, like an arrow leaving the bow. Beyond what we, with our insular outlook, regard as the dawn of civilization, must lie a long prologue, the ages of preparation. This is not to say that cultural development can be regarded as a slow but steady progress towards higher things. Certainly there have been thresholds of awakening and innovation – just as there have been stages in the decline and fall of different cultures. But the events which signalled new phases of development must have been preceded, almost without exception, by numerous experiments and a process of gradual, silent maturation. We are afforded only fleeting glimpses of a long journey. What we can see and touch are mostly things hewn in stone, painted on cave walls, or impressed in clay. Finds are often sporadic, and the meaning and application of many artefacts were perhaps not those that we assign them, as strangers blindly groping in another age. Much of what early man used in his cults and everyday life has not been preserved: wood has mouldered, bones have decayed, what was fashioned of earth and clay has often become one again with the soil. Most of the objects that have come down to us are fragments, plucked out of context. The vacuum surrounding them has to be filled by strivings for empathy – with the imagination that is opposed to fancy and that enables us to perceive echoes of the long prologue, some of them relatively clear, others more faint, some of them mystifying. We sense that there must have been voices which were later silenced, once they had made their contribution to the development of the race. Beyond the Babylonians, Egyptians and Greeks that Western man today reckons as his mentors one can surmise a whole cavalcade of mentors' mentors reaching far back into time. We begin to wonder whether some of what we now regard as recent discoveries were not in fact rediscoveries.

If one regards evolution as a flow in which everything at a given moment in time is conditioned by something else which went before, then the past becomes vitally important, both as a key to the present and a sketch-map of the future.

Here is a pole in the desert sand, where a creature of human shape moved some million years ago. We do not know whether early man was more or less intelligent than modern man; this is not something decided exclusively by brain volume. Our own advanced technology probably leads us to underestimate what human intelligence could achieve without our technical aids. Ultimately, of course, all our technologies can be traced back to the primary achievements of early man. It is possible that the intelligence revealed itself more in the original innovation than in its subsequent development.

Early man was biologically vulnerable, and was forced to compensate for this by his ingenuity. The sharply hewn chips of stone are a reflection of this ingenuity. Using these, the primate who had acquired a taste for meat could go a little beyond his own physical limits. Before a single spear had been sharpened, a single arrow threaded, or any bowstring twined, early man had probably been forced to compete with hyenas and vultures for the creatures brought down by lions and other great predators; these sharp stone tools were substitutes for the hyena's fangs and the vulture's beak, to slit through skin, hew flesh, and perhaps also to strip off slivers of hide.

No fossil can yet inform us who the toolmaker at man's first known settlement was. Was he a descendant, twelve hundred generations removed, of 1470? Or one of the near-humans that in two different versions lived in the lands east of the Great Water, only to disappear into silence. Conversely, no settlement has yet been found for 1470, who must be assumed to have been distributed along the whole length of the Valley and elsewhere in Africa. An intensive search is being carried out for such a settlement. It is reasonable to suppose that it will shift the manufacture of stone implements many hundreds of thousands of years backwards in time, and our horizons may be further displaced when the search is pushed on to find the common ancestors of 1470 and the near-humans.

No point will be found at which the beast became man. Even chimpanzees, after all, are capable of fitting straws together to catch termites in their nests, and making cones of leaves to carry water, and some have evidently been observed chipping stones – the old definition of man as the toolmaker is no longer valid. What distinguishes the human from the chimpanzee and from the near-human is perhaps the fact that he did not stop at the first chip of stone but carried his experiments further. That development, however, was spread out imperceptibly over long ages. Before the early hominids discovered how to use stones, they may have made simple implements and weapons of hard wood. Just as some hominids were early geologists and knew how to exploit the particular properties of different types of stone, so too they were probably aware of the variety of possibilities offered by different woods, and there may be an echo of this in the rich vocabularies certain African tribes use to describe trees, the names being linked with the various uses to which they can be put.

Man's biologically dictated inventiveness must also have taught him at an early stage to construct some sort of protection against other beasts of the earth. Too much importance has probably been accorded to caves as early human settlements, owing to the fossils and artefacts found in them. For the most part, early mankind's only resort was probably to construct shelters of twigs and branches: we can guess that they were slightly more advanced than those made by chimpanzees. Olduvai boasts the oldest man-made structure discovered to date: a ring built of hundreds of stones, large enough to have contained a clan of some twenty individuals – which is probably the maximum that could make a livelihood within a limited radius. This ring was obviously the base and support of a structure of branches and wicker forming a protective roof – and huts of this kind are still to be found in a number of remote areas in West Africa. The great number of bone and stone relics found outside the ring, and their complete absence inside it, indicate that the hut was used solely for shelter and as a place to sleep, all other activities being performed under the bare sky – which is the way many tribes still live. There are certain indications that the dwelling-place may have been enclosed by a stockade of thorn-bushes – the practice of the Massai, the Rendille and other tribes to this day.

Thus have primaeval techniques been preserved to our own day. The speed of the current has varied among different branches of the race. But retarded and advanced are experienced not as contrasts but simply as alternative conditions of life in this landscape, which so easily causes time to shrink.

Wilds and space – here in the Valley one experiences evolution both as a process and a direction. One has a sense of events marrying with each other, enabling a creature of the Valley to seek his way out over the planet, finally to reach out beyond its atmospheric covering. The way from the wilds out into space was opened up by the inventiveness that a biologically vulnerable creature was forced to develop in the struggle for survival. This same inventiveness was to leave deep marks on the planet which the creature from the Valley subsequently peopled.

I I

Back towards Koobi Fora, through this landscape of thorns and drought, flint and heat – a landscape that could be the beginning of the world, or its end.

It strikes me as perhaps the most monumental irony in history: the tract that saw man's birth, witnessed over several millions of years his groping search towards the future, transformed now into a wasteland, unpopulated and hostile.

Irony?

Or – a logical consequence?

12

You see them against the skyline, moving slowly across the great grasslands with their cattle. Their seamless, rust-red cloaks flutter around them, in their hands a rod or spear, its long, narrow tip flashing in the sun. They are as one with the movements of the herd. When the herd stops to graze they can stand for hours in their strange pose, like one-legged statues, the sole of one foot pressed against the opposite knee, leaning on their rod or spear.

Occasionally one of them detaches himself from the herd: his shape looms larger as he glides with long, low strides over the plain towards the camp. Once arrived, he stands for a while in silence, tall, incredibly slender, practically hipless, with firmly chiselled features, his right hand clasping his rod or spear while the left gently suggests that he would accept a glass of water. He thanks us with courtesy and rejoins the herd, which has begun to move and disappears after a time over the horizon.

A timeless picture of pastoral freedom, of Old Testament beauty.

The people we thus encounter are the Massai, those colourful Nilohamitic semi-nomads whose entire life is dictated by their love of zebu-cows and goats, convinced as they are that their god has given them the entire cattle population of the world as their heritage and never doubting for a moment their superiority to all other peoples. Four centuries ago they came pouring down from the north with their cattle and their weapons, their pride and their toughness, spreading over the entire Rift Valley from the Great Water to the area around Kilimanjaro.

As they move across the plain, they are a living illustration of Africa's history. The history of Africa is one of constant migrations.

If this is man's original home, then the migrations that finally spanned the globe must have started here. Even if the picture is by no means clear, the researchers believe they can trace how wave after wave of early humans left the Valley, and the tracts around the great lakes, seeking through Nature's own gateway a route down through the Nile Valley and out over Eurasia. The first emigrants may have been a race small in stature like 1470, or the pygmies of whom a few remnants have lingered on in the shadow of the African rain-forests.

Gates of exit were also gates of entry. Races which acquired their identity in the subsequent course of evolution, in the crucible of the Near East, returned to the continent of their origin. Group after group of Caucasian and Hamitic peoples seeped in over the Horn of Africa and through the gorges of Ethiopia.

On the continent of origin, evolution continued to fashion new racial patterns. From the Nile and its tributaries, Nilots and Nilohamites moved off towards the lands where 1470 and *Zinjanthropus* had lived. Other brews fermented in the Sahara, where a lush savannah, nourished by plentiful rain and criss-crossed with watercourses, nurtured a rich wild life and numerous human beings. When, fifteen thousand years ago, the ice began to withdraw across the frozen body of Europe, it was accompanied by the rain-bearing winds that had emptied water from the Atlantic over North Africa. The savannah withered in the waterless heat, the desert moved in and its human inhabitants were driven out; some found their way to the Atlantic coast of Europe, perhaps lending racial features to the

43

Bretons, the Welsh and the Irish, while the majority moved south, contributing to the Bantu peoples that were formed in the peripheral areas of the Congo basin and the Sahara Desert, and later spreading east and south to become a dominant theme in Africa's variegated racial fabric.

To the east the Bantu peoples encountered Arabs, who had filtered down along the coast, and East Asians, whom the monsoon winds had driven over the Indian Ocean; groups of Indonesians arrived with their plants, with yams and bananas that provided some substitute for what the desert had stolen.

Africa – a continent in continual movement. Its very geography, with its vast, almost oceanic grasslands, deserts and forests, invited travel. There were no sudden upheavals, as there were in the great Europe migrations. No Attila or Genghis Khan drove his hordes on with the violence of a prairie fire. Only a constant breaking camp, shifts in settlements stretching over generations, journeys to escape drought and find rain, from exhausted to virgin lands.

Tribes vanished, homogeneous groups were split, disparate groups united. The short-statured Dorobo, who as late as in this century collected wild honey and followed the trails of the shyest of creatures on the wooded slopes of Mount Kenya, lost both their language and their name. The bushmen, who talk to each other and to the beasts in an ancient language of clicking sounds, and in the Early Stone Age probably numbered a round million, were reduced to a scattered remnant on the edge of the Kalahari Desert. But the bushmen and the Bantu peoples, the Caucasians and the Nilots also mixed their blood with each other, producing the huge variety of tribes that is today one aspect of the African reality. It is estimated that a hundred thousand years ago this continent housed 125,000 people – probably more than any other. They are assumed to have been divided at that time into four main languages. Today, Africa's 400 million people speak over seven hundred different tongues.

"The land shadowing with wings". Such was Isaiah's description of Africa, crossed as it is by the equator. It was a country well known to the ancient peoples of the Middle East and the shores of the Indian Ocean as part of a dynamic cultural environment – while scarcely an echo had yet been heard from the restless warring tribes of Europe north of the Mediterranean.

Africa is ambiguous. What is different, what is contrasting is ever present – just as the shadow falls on either side. The traditional African community, which has survived more or less unchanged over the centuries, consists of small, coherent units, turned in upon themselves, their contacts restricted to their immediate surroundings and organized on a diffuse basis of equality, in a complicated interplay and counterplay between shepherds, farmers and hunters.

In many areas, however, migratory trails developed into routes for the exchange of goods and ideas with far distant places. When the Arabs brought the camel to Africa, its impact on the growth of trade was as great as when sails replaced oars at sea. At the tribal meeting-places and outside the traditional clan communities, empires developed which from an early age displayed strength and structure, pomp and circumstance.

There, mighty Ghana is founded where the caravan routes for salt and gold intersect. There, legend-wreathed Cush emerges on the Sudanese savannah, high along the course of the Nile, with its impassioned pyramid-builders and carvers of hieroglyphs long before the Egyptians had acquired these skills, and with its women swathed in colourful cottons from India and silk from China. There, the Queen of Sheba returns from King Solomon to her high mountains, with Judaism in her soul and a child in her womb – the two hundred and twenty-fifth heir of their encounter, the last Lion of Judah, was recently toppled from his throne. There, Chinese monsoon raiders strike their brown sails off the ocean coast to trade grey-green Sung ware and richly ornamented Ming for the carved ivory of the land of Pi-pa-lo. There, unknown engineers construct ingenious systems of irrigation and terracing that fill posterity with

45

admiration, while others raise granite columns higher than the obelisks of Egypt. There, the ruler of Mali fits out a grand expedition long before the days of Columbus to find out what is on the other side of the Atlantic. The universities in legendary Songhai and in Timbuktu become early intellectual centres.

And so they flicker past, a motley kaleidoscope of empires that rose, flourished, and vanished.

Further back emerge, as faint hints only, the well-nigh obliterated traces of still earlier cultures. In the rock paintings in Tassili-n-Ajjer in the Sahara, with their layer upon layer of pictures illustrating thousands of years of human history, we find among other things early versions of the Nile boat. An inscription in the temple of Horus at Edfu describes how Egyptian civilization came from the south with King Horus, whose followers were called the smiths – some anthropologists are convinced that African negroes were the first people to learn how to smelt iron, and that their art subsequently spread along man's ancient migratory routes to Europe and Asia. At Ngwnya in Swaziland, hematite was clearly mined over forty thousand years ago – for use in cosmetics!

Just as we can decipher long passages of our planet's history in the cosmic particles that have fallen on it down the ages, so too we owe to the heavens the opportunity to follow some of man's own doings. The radioactive carbon isotope C 14, which is formed in the higher strata of the atmosphere, and from there continuously showered down to earth, where it disintegrates according to a definite rhythm, makes it possible to date soil strata and objects sixty thousand years back in time. This little isotope may reshape our entire view of history. As we listen to its radioactive tick on our continent of origin, it may provide confirmation for those who have already had a presentiment and surprises for those who have not. Where man first appeared, there also we may find the origins of much of what we call civilization.

This was the continent that Hegel once proclaimed to be no

part of the historical world: "It has no movement, no progress to show". This was the continent that pale-skinned men from the north felt called upon to rescue from barbarity.

The physical nature of Africa throws man's migrations, and the divisions, separations and meetings of tribes into special relief. But Africa illustrates in broad outline what has happened on the globe of which man took possession. Much in the great pattern of migration is still diffuse. Along what tortuous paths were the genes carried that from this valley were to penetrate my own nursery, which had been fashioned by the Ice Age?

Soon, perhaps, we shall be able to follow with greater certainty the latest phase at least of man's constant migrations. With man went also pollen grains, the male sex cells of plants. Intentionally or unintentionally, the migrants took with them plant life from their previous settlements – in their own hands, or in the intestines of their cattle. Something of the terrain man had previously inhabited thus accompanied him. Where migrant seeds took root, pollen from the new plants filtered down year after year, century after century with the winds. Since the plastic sheaths of the pollen grains protect them from decomposition, it is possible, in plugs of earth, to follow not only the sequence of geological events, but also the nature and density of the vegetation at different times, and to see how forests have burned and given place to cereal grasses, and how new plants appeared.

The history of grasses becomes in some measure the history of man himself.

Possibly, the soil and grasses will one day give us a clearer picture of our own immediate origins, revealing perhaps links between the different sectors of the fragmented supercontinent which we are still unwilling to credit. As far as man's familiarity with wild cereals is concerned, our perspective back in time will in all certainty be pushed a good way beyond the earliest cultivations now known – beyond the fields of Jericho, beyond the Iranian highlands.

There is an air of timeless peace about the Massai as they move with their cattle slowly over the yellow grassland beneath the vast sky. They are a piece of history, living in the present: thus, hundreds and hundreds of generations of man have journeyed.

But as I watch the Massai who came up to our tent just now vanish with his cattle over the skyline, I know that he is also making his exit from history.

13

Over the African landscape, the soil spirals up in moving columns of dust. It is a fragment of African man himself that the wind is bearing off.

In the African's materially simple communities – which we in our technological short-sightedness regard as primitive – there was often a clear understanding of man's affinity with the earth. The earth was holy. No individual could own it. It was stewarded jointly, by a clan or a tribe many members of which were dead, some alive, and the great majority as yet unborn. The true title to it rested with those ancestors who had acquired it by a covenant with the earth-spirit when they took occupancy of the area. This was the foundation of the collectivist tradition that has permeated large parts of Africa.

This covenant with the earth-spirit gave the clan or the tribe its identity, history and security in an uncertain world. It legalized the territory, demanding in return reverence for the land itself. When the numbers of the clan or tribe increased so that a group had to leave and seek new land, the first task was to establish a cult site which symbolized the continuity with the group's ancestors and legalized the occupation of the new territory. If the land was taken from another clan or tribe, it was not always a brutally simple affair; it was expected of the invading group's leader that he should marry a daughter of the superseded group's chieftain, thus making his own clan party to the original occupants' covenant with the earth-spirit.

But in these societies, living close to nature, the affinity with the earth went still deeper. Evidence of this is to be found in the fossils of the human language: *humus* and *homo* have both evolved from the Indo-European word for earth, *dhghem*. Words that speak to us over the ages, myths that are still fresh today, rites repeated down through uncounted generations, all these go back to a primaeval concept of the earth mother. The earth was the belly from which the first man was born, after living as an embryo in its darkness.

The earth/generator and the woman/birthgiver embodied the same life-force. The woman's belly represented the darkness from which all life had emerged when it poured up from the womb of the earth – some dialects used the same word to denote the earth and the female vagina. The earth was a living female being, and the implements that tilled it were seen as male elements – in some languages, spade and phallus were designated by the same word. Also male was rain, which waters the earth and makes it fertile. Woman, on the other hand, who repeated the miracle of life, was regarded as being particularly close to the source of life. The earth's grasses and the hairs of the human body were equated with each other.

Man's connection with the earth was reflected in numerous birth-rites – the rite, after all, binds man to his total experience of life, just as the myth is rooted in the totality of man's condition. Women gave birth squatting close to the ground and its grasses; in this way the child was bound to its origin. The placenta, the umbilical cord and the child's first excrement were buried, according to widespread custom, near a tree or at a place where a tree was planted – in some tribes, people could point out the tree that had grown from their placenta.

Given this deep sense of affinity with the soil, death became a natural part of the life-cycle. The soil, from which life had sprung, received the dead as a self-evident preparation for new life. Decay was as natural a part of the life process of man as it was for the grass and the leaves. In certain tribes the dead man was laid out in the bush, shrouded in grass to re-unite him symbolically with the earth. The following night, the cries of the wild dogs and hyenas would be heard as they fought over the corpse – and if the dead man was not eaten up by the wild beasts it was taken as an evil omen. Committal to the beasts of the field rather than the worms of the soil was also a way of ensuring re-unification with the earth, and one practised by the Kikuyu down to the present generation.

Prior to the initiation, the magic hour of bleeding genitals when the youth's foreskin and the maiden's clitoris were slit with primitive knives, before the young were admitted to the traditions of the tribe and the secrets of life, the girls at least often dwelt for a time in a dark, silent seclusion which symbolized both a foetal existence and death. Admission to the adult world was a rebirth.

Reverence for the earth implies care. For the *kraal*, over which stood as a device and totem the smoke of its own camp-fire, the contours of the world were limited. Within its narrow compass, however, a constant proximity to nature had induced a view that was whole. The rhythm of life echoed that of nature. People's mystic sense of affinity with the land was combined with an exact and detailed knowledge of the properties of different woods and herbs, the habits of beasts, birds and insects. Such knowledge formed part of the clan's collective property. These simple human communities often lived in a relationship with their environment that might be described in the Norwegian philosopher Arne Naess's term "a life democracy" – or in the words of Basil Davidson, that fine connoisseur of African life, "a skilful interweave of the desirable with the possible".

Consideration was the key word – consideration for others within the collective and for the environment on which it depended. In a life lived close to the threshold of survival, no one could be allowed to take more than they needed, since they would be jeopardising the conditions necessary for the survival of the clan. An awareness that man could exercise too great a pressure on his resources was often interwoven in the African philosophies, as a sort of Malthusian pattern. Fragments from different myths reflect a concept of death at some point entering the world of man to prevent the multiplication of the species from causing permanent famine.

All this must stem from an intuitive wisdom and practical experience stretching deep back into the history of the species, with roots going back perhaps to pre-human times. An ecological message, if you will, communicated from generation to generation in countless removes.

Early man, like his hominid predecessors, had neither the ability nor the desire to make changes in his surroundings. He partook of the nutritional and water cycles and in the energy flow in the same way and on the same terms as other creatures. With the use of fire and the stone axe he acquired a new ability to influence the environment and the ability awakened also the desire.

A tribe whose pigment had faded beneath northern skies was to develop a culture which retreated more and more from the land and the soil, and all they stood for in symbolic terms. Even the Afro-Oriental cultures, which were closer to nature, began at an early stage to overexploit a soil that was particularly vulnerable in the tropics. In recent years, this wear has greatly increased.

Could it be that man's very feeling for the earth has been fossilized?

I watch the pillars of dust rise whirling from the landscape. As a child I used to wonder whether it should not be possible to see the wind. I can see it now. A wind brown and grey with the soil of Africa.

14

The last great migration into Africa was that of the white tribe. It occurred in the closing stages of a five-hundred-year power development in Europe.

It is true that the hunt for slaves, gold and spices had begun on the West Coast of Africa – both as an extension of the crusades and the beginning of a global process of expansion in which the lust of clerics for souls and that of adventurers for plunder were conjoined in a mostly amicable duality. But while Europe gradually filled the trade routes to America, the Orient and Australia with her sails, her nearest neighbour remained unknown, mysterious, an enigma. For four hundred years the Europeans were content to harry and to found trading stations on the Gold, Ivory and Slave coasts, halting on the shore-line, like the turtles of the sea. The only exceptions were the Boers, who pushed up from Capetown over the veld in pursuit of their Mosaic call, and challenged with their muskets the assegais of the Kaffirs in the struggle for pasturelands and water-holes.

The continent barricaded itself to the last against the white tribe, behind such defences as its structure afforded. To the north, the sand desert of the Sahara, which only the Arab and the Tuareg could navigate. To the east, the tsetse fly and the thick tangles of thorn, the fosse of the Rift Valley, and the Massai constituted a defence against encroachment. In the west, broad rivers emptied the waters of Africa into the Atlantic; they did not simultaneously lead upcountry, as is the manner of rivers, but entrenched themselves behind foaming cataracts and tangled mangrove roots. Behind these fortifications lay the terrors of fevers and snakes and tribes whose friendliness decreased the better they got to know the white man. Some sought their way into the deepest interior, few returned. When the rest of the globe had been more or less charted, the Nile, whose banks were lined with ancient cultures, still concealed the secret of its sources.

Sitting one evening in a camp beyond the common highway, with Mount Ngurunit glimpsed between luxuriant tree-tops, a parched river-bed before us along the bottom of which a party of Samburu are driving their goats, and a little white missionary outpost within reach, it is hard to believe that the Europeans pushed into the African interior a bare two lifetimes ago.

An old continent was a young acquaintance to the Europeans when they arrived: naturalists who were fired by Darwin to seek "missing links", "explorers" who were sometimes more concerned to promote themselves than the interests of science, missionaries profoundly concerned over the darkness pervading the souls of the blacks, adventurers enthused by the shining vision of a quick profit.

Once it had been opened up, Africa exercised the same kind of pull as does the sea upon those once forsworn to its cause. Some fell at the places they thought they were discovering. Others emerged with ruined health, cursing the land for its cruelty and the people for their savagery – only to go back into the bush.

The white paradox was how astoundingly little effort, considering how bewitched they were with the place, the whites made to understand Africa. To the gentleman explorer, the Africans were a means of crossing the continent or reaching the Mountains of the Moon, the sources of the Nile, and the Great

Water; the landscape often meant no more than an obstacle separating him from his goal.

His view of people of darker pigment was often coarse to the point of the exotic. The English "explorer" Richard Burton, who fiddled his instrument readings to locate Lake Tanganyika at a high enough altitude to be the source of the Nile, and who boasted to his drinking companions that he would bind one of his scabrous French tomes in skin flayed from a live negress, was able to claim in a so-called scientific context that the African had failed to develop from the primitive to the less primitive because he lacked the mental qualifications for civilization. Sir Samuel Baker observed that the soul of the African people was "as inert as the swamps that comprise their wretched world". Stanley shot natives the way he shot monkeys.

Extreme cases – but illuminating. How the Africans experienced the coming of the white man, no one ever asked. The whites themselves measured Africa by European standards. Their expeditions and settlements were small fragments of Europe, governed by the laws, conventions and prejudices of Europe, and they had no interest in seeking contact with African communities on their own terms. No dialogue that might have rendered fruitful the re-uniting of the tribes after their long separation was thus possible. Europe's encounter with Africa was characterized by the unquestioned dogma of white superiority and black inferiority. This dogma was used to justify a mode of behaviour characterized by much brutality and a little philanthropy – both, as a rule, equally misdirected. Having destroyed the natives' life-pattern and shattered their fragile cultures, the Europeans could honestly believe what they wanted to believe – that Africa had never had any civilization. Colonization could thus be presented as a civilizing mission. When the Europeans made the trade in human flesh a large-scale industry, any sense of guilt could be anaesthetized by the comforting knowledge that the African was a slave by nature – for the simple reason that he allowed himself to be enslaved.

"The less intelligent the white man, the more stupid he found the black", observed André Gide. The Europeans measured not only the African but also his land in their own way. The continent was parcelled out on the drawing-board between different states, without regard to geography, demography, or ancient routes of communication.

The good land was divided up among the white immigrants. Tribal communities were broken up, clans that had little in common were lumped together, villages were separated from their pasture-lands. In Kenya some of the best highland areas were reserved for the white immigrants, becoming the "White Highlands" in the black man's country. The white tribe also penetrated the Valley, which had seen so many tribes come and go since the man first appeared there. A British High Commissioner was concerned to add an entirely new page to the chequered history of the Valley by turning the whole bed of the Valley from Mount Kenya to Lake Tanganyika into the "White Lowlands". The Africans were barred from the lands accorded to their ancestors by the earth spirit, and assigned homes in native reservations. The Massai were robbed of the greater part of their nomad kingdom. The Kikuyu were forced down from their mountains to provide casual labour for European farmers in the Valley. Africans were forbidden to cultivate potatoes or coffee.

Just as the white invaders regarded the good land as theirs, so too they considered they had a right to the gold, diamonds, tin and copper that earlier geological events had packed into the earth-crust. The Africans themselves comprised a natural resource that could be used as cheap labour on farms and in mines: the philosophy of the slave trade applied to the blacks' own continent.

Previous invasions had produced fusions. Now, two worlds met which failed to fuse. Perhaps because the white tribe had grown too remote from their common origins. The English, dressed in hunting pink, still rode to hounds, and made no more effort than the Boers to conceal the fact that apartheid was a necessary condition of their colonial system. The French and the Portuguese erected no racial barriers *in principle*. Everyone, in the French colonies, was accepted as a French citizen – which meant learning the French language, French history, and reverence for *la gloire de la France*. Portugal's colonies were regarded as part of metropolitan Portugal: everyone could become a Portuguese citizen who became "civilized". Which was to say learned to speak and think Portuguese and genuflect before the white Madonna: by the time Portugal finally gave up, after four hundred years of industrious "civilizing", just under one per cent had become citizens of their own country.

While fifteen generations of whites turned North America into a predominantly white continent and a launching pad for their space craft, the whites in Africa never succeeded in more than splashing the surface with their colour. What they did achieve was to ram Africa back a century or so in its tracks.

And they did something more, too. They left their mark on the land. And on people's minds.

There were, of course, tribes that came into very little contact with the colonizers. But those who became dependent on them were constantly reminded of their physical and moral degradation in a way that tended to erode their self-respect. Humiliated, robbed not only of their fields but also of their gods, their life-form and their life-rhythm, in exchange for European values and European gew-gaws, millions of Africans were precipitated into a crisis of identity. Worse than the physical consequences of the slave trade, which furnished the Caribbean and the two Americas with fifteen million slaves and cost a further thirty or forty million Africans their lives, worse than scattered kraals, depopulated territories and the plundering of the continent's natural resources were the spiritual consequences of the era of white dominion. It left a legacy that still obscures the European's picture of the African, and persists in the African as an uncertainty, a vulnerability, and a smouldering mistrust of the white man.

15

An unknown wood-carver of the Makonde tribe has fashioned a number of figures, which Professor Mascarenhas shows me in his workroom at the university in Dar es Salaam. I have never before seen anything that portrays the situation of mankind with such awful simplicity. With a blend of symbolism and realism they communicate the reality of hunger. There are the characteristic marks of starvation: thin limbs, swollen stomachs, terror in the eyes. One distorted figure seems to be eating earth, another his own hand. These figures have, simultaneously, the shapes of human beings and animals, as if to emphasize that all life exists on the same terms.

These images pursue me when we continue our journey. Africa fills with dust during the dry period. The dust trails after our landcruiser like the tail of a comet, rises in clouds around the hoofs of the cattle, and forms small puffs of smoke around the beaks of birds as they peck at the ground. When whirls of dust then rise from shimmering waves of air over the naked ground, they assume in my eyes the form of distorted human figures.

When people die, bells are rung, muffled drums are beaten, lamentations are heard. No bell rings, no drums are heard, no wailers are to hand when the wind blows away a piece of loosened earth. Yet that is the fatal moment.

Droughts and rains have always succeeded each other. We can follow the changes in climate millions of years back through the altered positions of the lake shores in the landscape over the ages, and through the different strata in the sediment. In Olduvai, two great periods of drought are thought to have occurred during the last million years, one 700,000, the other 150,000–300,000 years ago. The picture obtained from Koobi Fora is not entirely similar, but agrees in its essentials. Differing frequencies of pollen reveal how the vegetation was impoverished during the great droughts. The fossil relics of hominids and animals during such periods are scarce to the point of non-existence.

Within such large-scale shifts in climate, minor fluctuations occur. Twenty thousand years ago the Sahara extended further south than it does now – before wet millenia arrived and the desert flowered once more.

In the arid and semi-arid areas south of the Sahara, a severe drought is part of the experience of every generation, marking an era in much the same way as the world wars do for Europeans. The droughts are given names. Somalis speak of *Xaaraamacune* (1911–12), "The eater of forbidden food", when the faithful were forced to eat what is prohibited by Islam; *Siigacase* (1950–51), "The blower of red dust", the drought of the sand storms; and most recently *Dabadheer*, "The long-tailed one", which has lasted so many years.

The drought that has persisted since 1968 is spoken of as the worst in human memory. But ample testimony is available to the incessant advances of the desert over the past seventy or more years. Among the Turkana, who live at the lowest limits at which the human body can survive, driving their cattle over the dunes on the western shore of the Great Water, and still believing that the world ends on the eastern side, the older men recall how in their boyhood the area was green with trees and grass, and how rhinoceroses, buffaloes, giraffes and zebras roamed there. Now the savannah is gone, and with it the great beasts; only a few hardy hyenas and the black-maned desert lions circle around the villages and herds. The same story as is told in Turkanaland is repeated monotonously elsewhere.

All this raises the question whether we are entering a new geological period of drought, or whether the new deserts are entirely the work of man. We do not, as yet, have the sort of overview that permits a final answer. Certain researchers believe there are signs that we are at the beginning of a long-term, global climatic change that will produce persisting drought throughout the equatorial belt, from Africa over the Indian sub-continent to the western hemisphere.

If this interpretation is correct, the fossil-less strata in Olduvai and Koobi Fora assume an ominous meaning. And, indeed, an American biologist has drawn the drastic conclusion that the entire Sahel area south of the Sahara should be evacuated and an international apparatus set up to take care of its people.

Regardless of how nature's primaeval forces operate, man is present as a new geological factor. In nature, things happen without purpose but never without cause. Man has become a cause. He can affect the conditions of life on this planet as much as the continental drift and the eruptions of volcanoes. He cannot avoid a long-term deterioration of the climate. But he can magnify and aggravate it, and he can prolong what might otherwise have been transitory. And he can cause his own deteriorations in the climate.

Yellow, worn plains, timeless scenes of herds and cattle, soil cut asunder and rising in clouds around sharp hooves! For thousands of years the herdsman followed his beasts from pasture to pasture. He adopted the same pattern as the herbivores on the savannahs. During the rainy season, the beasts of the savannah disperse to pastures around temporary streams and heads of water: in the dry season they draw together round the permanent waterholes. Some species undertake seasonal migrations resembling those of birds.

We stood recently in Masai Mara, watching the magnificent spectacle as hundreds of thousands of gnus set out on their annual trek from the steppes of Serengeti in Tanzania to the

Narok plain in Kenya. They were like an army on the march: column after column appeared on the southern skyline, column after column vanished below the horizon to the north. A biological clock had signalled their departure before any rain clouds could be seen, so that they could reach their new pastures by the time the monsoons came, with their life-giving wetness.

As one stands in the midst of this primaeval spectacle the image also comes to life of people over the ages decamping from the regions that had been struck by drought. Their ranks are joined by the army of a million people that the drought in Sahel recently drove out in a desperate quest for food. But, above all, these gnus on the move afford a reminder of natural forces that for thousands of years also determined the movements of nomad peoples. Their life path lay between droughts and rains. Their herds were travelling larders, in which the herdsman stored food for the lean years that he knew would come. The more the herd grew, the greater was his security. In a similar way, the early farmer accommodated himself to the laws of his environment. He knew that if the baobab tree failed to bloom in October the harvest would be poor; at the same time, his adaptation to the properties of the soil and the reality of the drought was embedded in his whole pattern of life.

The nomad's once well contrived system of stewarding the gifts of nature is now becoming his enemy. The number of people has increased, as has the number of cattle. What was previously a reasonable desire to increase the herds has been driven beyond the bounds of reason. During half a man's lifetime, the number of people and cattle in the areas bordering the Sahara has doubled, in both north and south. The grazing cattle are twice as many as the grass can feed when times are hard. Nowhere in the world is there any longer any unexploited, free grazing land, least of all in Africa. As the land along the southern edge of the Sahara is overgrazed and destroyed, people and herds move southwards to areas already overcrowded. And thus the closing scenes of a story dating back many thousands of years are played out!

The colonial era expedited the overworking of Africa's soil. When the white settlers took the best land, the Africans were pushed away to thin, marginal soils, far too fragile to sustain the pressure to which they were subjected. Also, the traditional pattern of agriculture was disrupted, in that the settlers favoured crops affording but poor protection against the burning sun and heavy rains of the tropics. Many of the free African countries are continuing to cultivate the white man's cash crops to barter for the white man's industrial products. And so the white pressure on the soil of Africa is maintained.

A couple of days at Baringo – in blast-furnace heat and an air thick with dust – gives a harrowing picture of how quickly soil can be misappropriated. Lake Baringo is one of the few fresh-water lakes in the Valley, free from the volcanic soda that accumulates in the lakes that are not drained. As recently as fifteen years ago its water was crystal-clear. Ten years ago it was becoming slightly turbid. Today it is as brown as chocolate blancmange. The reason becomes painfully evident as one travels along the lake. When the whites left the shores they had previously monopolized for their recreation, tribes of herdsmen moved in with their cows and goats. The grass was grazed down to its bare scalp, and sharp hooves bereft the roots of their purchase. In an incredibly short time, large areas have been transformed into lifeless red-brown desert. When the rains come, great volumes of loose earth are flushed into the lake. The land and the lake are the same colour.

What we cannot see is the soil that is also flushed down from the deforested sides of the valley during the three months the river-beds carry water. We know, however, that the tropical forests are being felled at an alarming rate, and that the rains which previously filtered gradually down through the foliage and reached the ground as a kindly drizzle now assail the ground with something like hostility, tearing away the soil.

Earth that is stripped naked, bereft of its green cloak! Here, at last, is a small patch of grass by a depression in a dried-up river-bed, inviting to rest and thought. Hundreds of millions of years ago, grasses and herbs moved in over previously naked continents. Slowly, over more millions of years, they created the remarkable blend of previous life that is the topsoil. Every blade of grass grows from the mould that its predecessors helped create. In a way, the history of life is contained in the blade of grass you are holding in your hand. When the topsoil is dispersed and the grass dies, a large part of the history of which man is a product vanishes with it.

Baringo provides a picture in miniature of what is now happening on the grand scale. Savannahs become steppes, the steppes become deserts. More than two-fifths of Africa's surface is covered today by deserts, semi-deserts, and dry bushland – much of it manmade. In the same way, great parts of Southern Asia and Latin America are losing arable land to the desert.

As we left Koobi Fora and travelled through the Chalbi desert, we were reminded several times of the force with which the sand makes its onslaught. Where some clump of grass, some bush or tree by the edge of the desert holds back the heavier particles that the wind drives along the ground, the sand collects in an ever-growing drift, enveloping the plant and choking it. Until finally, perhaps, only a dry, twisted branch sticks up from the crown of the slope by way of epitaph. The desert has won, the sand dunes move forward – as they once moved over Jericho and Babylon, Troy and Carthage.

The Sahara is growing at a rate of over 250,000 acres a year. Not along a coherent front, but by patches of desert forming in the steppe areas, patches that spread until they merge into each other. From the air, you can see how the landscape seems to be bleeding from open wounds, where the rust-red earth has been laid bare.

The fine dust of topsoil and nutrients is lifted by the wind to a height of over three miles and carried out over the Atlantic and Indian Oceans. From satellites, photographs have been taken of dust clouds stretching from Africa to the Caribbean. Some parts of North Africa have lost up to a foot of their topsoil in the space of five years. In Barbados, in the Caribbean, measurements show that the amount of dust borne by the wind has increased fourfold in seven years. The connection is unmistakable.

Anders Rapp, the Swedish expert on the dry areas of Africa, has calculated that during a mere six months in the summer half of the year, sixty million tons of fine earth particles were blown out over the Atlantic just from Sahel. If all this was topsoil, and we assume that the topsoil in the arid areas is often no more than a few inches thick, it would mean that every summer well over 200 square miles of arable land in these areas are literally gone with the wind. Such an area of arable land would afford pasture for 6,000–10,000 head of cattle. It could also feed perhaps 60,000 people whose nourishment came directly from the soil.

The wind that should carry water from the sea to the continents, is carrying soil from the continents to the sea. It will one day be possible to read in the sediment on the bed of the Atlantic the story of man's responsibility for man's starvation.

16

In the evening after a dusty day we pitch our tent by the Rendille tribe's waterhole on the edge of the Kaisut desert. Night falls quickly. Inzoka and Ndambuka move like silent shadows by the fire as they prepare the evening meal.

The firmament is impressively close and incredibly clear. We linger for a long time outside the tent, following the serene process of the constellations over the desert. There, we see the Pleiades. For some cattle-breeding peoples, the return of the Pleiades is a promise that the white monsoon clouds are not far away. The Pleiades are the heralds of the rain, like the buds of the baobab tree and certain migratory birds.

One has to come close to drought and thirst fully to realize what rain means. Much of what may otherwise seem picturesque then acquires a deeply human import. People kneeling at the roots of a fig tree with entreaties and burnt offerings to some deity whom it is thought can lead the clouds like streams of water. Drums telegraphing their *ndaandi ndaandi* – the leader of the clan summons its members to a meeting when the signs of rain have failed, so that they can decide whether they should look for some evil black magic within the clan or send messengers to a reputable rainmaker. Rain dancers in a primaeval ritual in which they may or may not believe, but which has to be performed, much as the Catholic lights his candle before the image of the saint. People attaching grass to their clothing to adjure the rain: the rain that is to give life to the grass – the grass that is to feed the cattle – the cattle that are to feed man.

Morning in the desert. A cloudless morning. The Pleiades fail to redeem their promise. Neither this day – nor the next – nor the following day. Something has gone wrong up there, something against which neither the rainmaker's conjurations nor the silent prayer by the fig tree are of avail.

As the sun rises, families of Rendille with their camels and goats come to the waterhole in the dry river-bed. The women's water containers of giraffe hide stands like amphoras in the sand while they fetch water for the animals. Another of these timeless scenes: Rachel at the well.

The men describe to us how it has become necessary to dig the wells deeper and deeper. They also tell us that some groups of Rendille, when it is most dry, drive their camels all the way to the Great Water, the brackish lake. When the camels get the scent of the water in their nostrils they set off at the run with their slack bellies and humps flapping, rush out into the water, and drink until their bellies and humps swell out like balloons before staggering ashore, full of water that will last them as many days as a man has fingers.

But here, at the Rendille's waterhole, everything takes place quietly and with dignity. The camels retain their air of superiority, the desert people their serenity. What happens at the well is a rite. When it has been performed, the Rendille move on. People and animals are visible for a moment against the desert sky – the camels laden with the water-bags and simple belongings of the people.

The price we pay in the industrialized countries for only having to turn a tap to obtain water is the loss of any sense of water's nature and value. For people who live close to a sometimes parsimonious nature, water is not just a chemical compound. It is a fluid as full of mystery as blood, with the same vital force as semen. It seems at times as if these people lived in a secret understanding with the flood that has born evolution onward, the flood that flows through the arteries of the soil and through the veins of the leaves and the sinews. As if their own roots, like those of the grass, were seeking the moisture, in the depth of the mould.

In the arid and semi-arid areas – and these comprise four-fifths of Kenya and over half of Tanzania – it is the proximity of a more or less permanent source of water that determines where man can settle. People often have to go a long way to satisfy their need of water. One of the characteristic features of the African landscape is the constant movement of the women to and fro with water jars on their heads or in a harness on their backs.

Just as the level of the water is sinking in the desert wells, so too the lakes in the Valley are shrinking. This has happened before, but there is still something desolate in seeing the shorelines retreat at an observable rate. Lake Nakuru, where a million or so flamingoes used to seek their images in the water, has fallen about four feet in one year. When we visited Nakuru, all the flamingoes had left the stage. Instead we found them in Baringo and up by the Great Water, the first time they had appeared there. But the Great Water is also retreating, year by year. To the north, the River Omo is forming a delta with the sludge from the eroded mountainsides of Ethiopia, a delta that it is believed will fill the entire upper half of the lake in two or three lifetimes. Its sister lake, Lake Stefani, once clear, has become a fen. Will the Great Water meet the same fate?

When the regular resources fail – as during the latest drought – both animals and people seek desperately for other expedients. Elephants root up their own wells in the sand to get deep enough to reach the water with their trunks; when they have gone, the buffaloes and birds come to collect any drops that may be over. People trekking from the parched areas hold out their empty water vessels in dumb appeal to these they encounter. Water becomes a commercial product. In some places, a cask of water attracts the price of a sheep. For how many others is that cask of water to suffice, and for how long?

The governments draft ambitious programmes to ensure that every family will have access to clean water within a decade (Tanzania), or by the turn of the century (Kenya). When we know that half the world's population lacks access to clean water, we can sense the breadth of such promises. Experts doubt that these water programmes can keep pace with the increase in population. Kenya, which at present has a population of 13 million, is expected to have 30 million by the turn of the century, and Tanzania, with 15 million now, also 30 million, while the whole of Africa, which now has a population of 400 million, will have increased to 800 million. New mouths to feed, new thirst to quench – a task of incredible dimensions.

The subsoil water would appear to be sufficient for the people and the cattle, say the spokesmen of WHO, but not for irrigation. It renews itself only very slowly – in the areas around Nairobi only two or three per cent of the raincatch reaches the subsoil water. It is expensive to get at, and often has to be sought at a depth of some hundred and fifty metres. The governments of Africa, supported by international aid, drill and construct hydrants. Such projects are often ecological disasters because they are not incorporated in any coherent ecological programme. When new hydrants are opened, the herds of cattle are driven there, increase to the limit of what the new water suffices for, and soon wear out the grazing land around the hydrant so that it becomes desert. It has happened that tens of thousands of cows have died in the proximity of the life-giving water because the grass had been grazed out of existence. With supreme irony, the water proved the death of the grass.

All that we see with our eyes, even so, are but details in a large and elusive pattern. What the nomad at the hydrant does not realize and what people in the industrial world would, it seems, prefer not to know is that both together may be triggering cosmic forces that it will one day be impossible to master.

In nature, fresh water undergoes a constant cycle. The sea, the sun and the atmosphere form a gigantic wheel, which keeps the water in continual circulation: from the sea to the atmosphere, from the atmosphere to the continents, and from the continents back to the sea. About 25 cubic miles of the water vapour lifted from the oceans by the sun every year is emptied as rain over the continents: the same amount returns to the sea via the subsoil water and rivers – the circle has then been completed, the wheel has turned once.

When the world population has doubled, shortly after the year 2000, the artificial irrigation of thirsty areas will increase sharply. Insofar as man is unwilling to empty the reservoirs of subsoil water that past ages have stored in the earth's crust, he must try to retain as much as possible of the water that the clouds empty over the continents. However, a high proportion of the water that is collected in dams and used to irrigate the fields evaporates and never reaches the sea: this applies above all in the tropical belt, where the percentage of evaporation in some places is estimated to be up to five times greater than actual precipitation. The more such evaporation increases, the more the global circulation of water is affected. A Russian scientist has calculated that if the amount of water that runs from the land surface back into the ocean is reduced by two per cent, then this – *ceteris paribus* – would cause the sea level to drop two hundred and fifty metres – admittedly over a period of forty thousand years.

The reality, of course, will be more complicated. It is already more complicated. It is suspected that in the short term it will be the oceans that furnish increasingly less water to the continents.

Several researchers believe that the clouds of dust drifting over the oceans are disturbing the exchange of energy between the sea and the atmosphere, reducing the production of water vapour that takes place when the rays of the sun meet the sea. A Swedish plant biologist has complemented the picture with a second theory that the steadily increasing amounts of carbon dioxide vomited out into the atmosphere by the industrialized countries can trigger off a chain of reactions in the sea: the carbonic acid liberates nutrient salts, the nutrient salts increase the production of algae, the light-pigmented algae reflect an increasing amount of the sunlight that falls; in this way, the oceans are acquiring less energy for evaporation. In both cases the result is that the low pressures would be enfeebled, and drop their rain on the threshold of continents instead of carrying it in over the land.

A third theory, developed by the American workers Bryson and Macload, is if possible still more ominous in what it portends. This theory starts from the currents of air from north and south which run together at the equator. Their place of meeting over the African continent moves northwards during the spring and summer, southwards during the winter. On the northern side of the front where these currents meet, the rising high pressure gives birth to the hot, dry north-eastern wind known as the Harmatta, the very breath of the desert. Where it meets the moist south-westerly monsoon, the humidity is normally pressed together in cumulus clouds, which bless the ground with their rain. When the monsoon is laden with dust from a dry earth, it no longer reaches as far north as previously, and the formation of clouds is hindered. The rain then fails to appear in the Sahel belt, or loses its force. The first implication of this theory is that drought breeds drought. But the dust from the dried-up soils of Africa is joined by air pollution from the industrialized countries. Above all, their rapid consumption of the oil that was once packed into the crust of the earth, for example where Africa, Arabia and Eurasia collided, is tending to force back the rain-bearing monsoons. The poor in their poverty, the rich in their hectic quest for economic growth, both are helping to increase the drought and thirst in the poor countries. That is the theory's second implication.

As yet, nothing can be demonstrated with certainty. But the suspicions have been voiced. That is disturbing enough. Let us think what we mean by a "trigger effect". The effect by which a man can bring down an elephant by crooking the forefinger of his right hand. In a similar way, apparently small acts can have great, perhaps irreversible consequences for the global climate.

Something has caused the Pleiades to renege on their promise. Perhaps the world's own great waterwheel, which has developed a fault.

17

New camp sites, where we are alone with the beasts of the forests, the savannahs and the grasslands.

The crater lake at Marsabit, where the rain forest hangs like a green tapestry around the edge of the crater. Elephants setting laboriously about their evening toilet, having come down to the lake to drink and wash down their bodies with water and dust, raising their trunks like curved horn instruments as they trumpet to the mountainsides. Buffaloes sluggishly moving in the edges of the lake from dusk to dawn. A kudu antelope with great spiralled horns gliding past the opening of the tent. A lion on its nightly round of inspection in the camp.

The bottom of Ngorongo's vast caldera, which during the day is one of Africa's great tourist attractions; at night, we are alone in our tent under a fig tree, with the world's greatest concentration of wild beasts around us, in a darkness filled with sounds.

The savannah by the fast-shrinking salt-lake of Ndutu, with Serengeti's vast seas of grass nearby. Our closest neighbours a few giraffes – the name comes from the Arabic *zurafa*, which so adequately means mild. Their heads sway gracefully above the tree-tops, the only sound they make is a short sigh from their long throats. The plain itself is polka-dotted with thousands upon thousands of impalas, Grant's and Thomson's gazelles, gnus, kongoni antelopes and elands. A panorama of life, the details of which are constantly new, but which as a whole is constantly repeated: search and flight, copulation, birth and death – with death as a tremendously self-evident component of the life-pattern.

These are the pictures of indescribable beauty. Nowhere else in the world does one find such a wealth of species, such a multitude of wild beasts as in the game reserve in the Valley and its vicinity.

The contrast with the manmade deserts from which we have just come is enormous, the journey between a ruined landscape and pristine luxuriance almost shockingly brief.

Only a couple of centuries ago, all Africa teemed with wild animals, incorporated in and expressing the continent's shifting conditions of life. They formed a huge ecological interplay, which included man. African tribes tended to direct their spears more against each other than the wild beasts, killing animals as a rule only for food, in self-defence, and for ritual purposes. The early Arabian trade in ivory had little effect on life in the wilds. Then came the Europeans, with their crucifix, whisky, and fire-arms, and the extermination of species began in earnest. South Africa lost the greater part of its large mammals when the Boers pushed up over the veld with their waggon trains. Then, when the white tribe, a hundred years ago, forced the barrier behind which the African interior had hitherto concealed its mystery and its wealth, a great part of the continent was transformed into a slaughterhouse.

Stanley worked out that if one were to shoot the 200,000 elephants of the Congo basin, obtaining an average 50 pounds of ivory per head, one would have acquired ivory worth 5 million pounds sterling – mainly for use in billiard balls. In actual fact, two million elephants were shot in Africa in the thirty years around the turn of the century. There, at least, the profit motive was an excuse. Otherwise, it was often enough for a white man to see an animal for his rifle to go up to his shoulder.

During the Second World War, white soldiers shot from their jeeps at anything that moved in the bush, not for gain but simply in order to kill.

In sixty years the number of wild animals was reduced by three-quarters, the greatest slaughter in world history. Vast areas of the African landscape were emptied of big game. What remains is still a world of stark experiences. To meet this multitude of creatures in their natural surroundings, to feast one's eyes and soul on their physical beauty, the perfection of their movements, to see how the biological systems merge in each other like waves so that each species is able to exploit its part of their common habitat – all this is to return to a world of seething evolutionary activity, as it must have functioned during the earliest days of the human race. And perhaps it was precisely here, in the crater country around Ngorongoro and on the savannahs of Serengeti that man took the step from passive eater of carrion to active hunter.

The game survives in relative density only in various reserves and national parks. It survives only as long as man permits.

But it is increasingly threatened. Poaching – with snares and pitfalls, poisoned arrows and machine-guns – is on a scale that would hardly be possible without protection high up, very high up, in certain administrations. It is seldom the meat that is wanted: the tails of giraffes are made into flyswatters, the rhinos are hunted to death because their horns, which in fact are not horns but thickenings of the skin, can be ground into a powder that Indian superstition believes improves sexual prowess; the elephant still satisfies the desire of the whites for ivory ornaments (and billiard balls); the leopard, the silent shadow and personification of the tropical night, provides luxurious furs for the women of the white tribe.

A growing population and devastated soils will increase the pressure on those pleasure gardens that remain. Not even Serengeti is an enclosed ecological unit: the life rhythm of many of its beasts carries them away from the park for long periods.

It is these environments that are now, primarily, being occupied. However, the infiltration has started in a couple of areas within the actual reserve. So far, they have been saved by the revenues from the tourist trade – but more tourists also mean more wear and tear. And what government, in the long run, is capable of holding the barrier between the animals and human hunger?

Salvation could lie in a regulated out-take of game, just as elk hunting in the Nordic forests is subject to quotas and licences. The wild herbivores, who have driven the sharing of nutritional resources so far that some twenty different species can graze in the same area without competing, permit a vastly greater biomass per given area than domestic cattle. In that a long evolutionary process has incorporated them in a symbiosis with the grass and the trees, they also keep the savannahs and grasslands alive. No deserts are created by the zebras and giraffes.

The game available could still man's hunger more efficiently and on a more permanent basis than zebus and goats – if reason were to prevail. As it is, the pleasure of experiencing life in the wilds is tinged with melancholy. It is difficult to escape the feeling of belonging to a privileged generation, perhaps the last, perhaps the next last that can experience this wild life in its own environment. Any evening after a long day in the wilds, it is as if you saw the creatures of another age chasing off towards the dying fire of the sun.

When one sees how our species is trampling underfoot the fragile network of dependences and impulses that binds all life together, the best one can wish is not that mankind should become more human but that he should become more animal. When mankind no longer has place for creatures together with whom he has developed over millions of years, then it is possible that Nature will no longer have room for mankind.

18

To travel in Africa today is to travel in two worlds. The old and the new appear in contrast, often in dramatic relief.

Tribal conditions, rooted in the primaeval origins of the race, are still alive. This is particularly true in the Valley and its surroundings. To meet the Massai, the Samburu, the Turkana and the Rendille is to meet a pattern of life many thousands of years old.

Originally, after all, all men were nomads: first came the hunters and gatherers, then the herdsmen. Today, a dwindling percentage of humanity follows the old way of life. Some of these people are to be found in mankind's original home.

Just as the savannah and the billowing grasslands perhaps saw the appearance of the first huntsman, so too must they have invited, early on, a pastoral style of life. And where should it have survived if not in this countryside?

The earth belonged to no man, and thus to all – such was the wisdom of the nomads. They had few private possessions, as was inherent in their way of life. The pattern persisted when nomads became farmers. The clan – whether consisting of hunters, herdsmen or farmers – totally enclosed the individual. The collective afforded external protection in return for which it was allowed to regulate the individual's entire path through life. The collective let everyone decide, but disposed in its turn over the individual: this afforded psychological security, but it also exercised a strong pressure on each man. The individual was an integral part of the clan, as he was of the natural environment that was the clan's world. It was the collective that gave him his identity.

Songs and tales, maxims and religious concepts, the entire tradition that emerged from the clan's or the tribe's specific conditions, was summed up in what we can call an oral literature. This too was a collective work, the common property of the clan or tribe. Preserved from generation to generation, constantly retold around the camp fire, it gave the clan or tribe a long memory.

A community of this kind, particularly if it is tied to the limitations of a specific environment, is little inclined to change. The tradition conserved. Now, the very foundation of pastoralism is being eroded. The herdsman, with all he has given the race of spaciousness, and spiritual freedom, is leaving the stage.

The Massai and the Rendille have become the captives of the shrinking grasslands and expanding deserts. They are out of step with the age. Even where they still cling to the old way of life, something of their inner clarity has become clouded, their sense of independence has been shaken.

The event that more than any other ripped apart the old tribal pattern was, of course, the arrival of the white tribe. With their zeal in spreading their religious beliefs and mass-produced wares, and above all by their encouragement of individual effort at the expense of the collective, the Europeans radically influenced subsequent development. Even now that they have withdrawn, their footprints still mark the sand.

Africa's explosion into formal independence entailed copying, within the arbitrary frontiers drawn up by the colonial powers, the European nation state – and that at a time when the nation state had outlived its usefulness. An Africa chequered by frontiers decreed not by Africans but by Europeans was almost bound to provoke those antagonisms we call tribal warfare in the African, but nationalism in the European, context. From the Europeans the Africans also took over administrative and – insofar as they existed – educational systems. The imitation of Europe appeared to set the seal on the continent's freedom. But the patterns imitated were poorly suited to African traditions and premises. What appeared to be a poor start on the part of Africa, was the legacy of Europe.

Even if the names of whites on coasts, mountains and territories are fast being erased, they sometimes linger on, revealingly. When the Europeans came to the highlands east of the Rift Valley, they heard the area spoken of by the Kikuyu, the "fig-tree people", as *Keere-Nyaga*, the Kikuyu phrase for the white streaks on the mountain in the heart of the area. To European ears the name sounded like Kenya – the European mistake lives on in the name of the liberated African state.

The white tribe brought the written language to Africa. But the written language was English or French. It was by nature individualistic and could not, as had the oral tradition, epitomize the jigsaw-puzzle pieces of numerous spiritually related but anonymous contributors. Parallel with more concrete political measures, the written language became a means of severing the traditional ties which bind the tribes. Since the tribal languages are limited (although Swahili is winning ground), modern African writers are compelled to write in the language of the former colonial powers, even when their purpose is to assert what is specifically African. But a language reflects a cultural posture, and they adopt imperceptibly with the language something of the white tribes' scale of values.

By various sophisticated means, the white tribe still retains its cultural and economic grip on the continent. While Africans guard the frontiers laid down by the Congress of Berlin, multinational corporations are quietly dividing the country up into new spheres of interest. This neo-colonialism is facilitated by the fact that the course taken by the whites has come, for many people in the poor countries, to stand for economic and technical progress.

All this has produced a dichotomy in the communities of Africa, and in people's hearts. Many Africans today live in a duality as the children of two worlds, torn between two life forms which impinge upon each other, with their conceptions and misconceptions, their hopes and their dreams, their strengths and their weaknesses. Much of the songs and the visions, the customs and the rites that once sprang from a total human situation still retain their grip. Much again has lost its meaning, or is languishing fast. When the ritual dances with the lions' manes, the ostrich feathers, the throats bubbling with bird-calls, have lost their original meaning and become something displayed for money to tourists, it is understandable if many of the younger people turn in shame from the tribal traditions – to which, even so, they may still secretly cling, while outwardly copying Western customs. The pressure of the clan has eased but a certain element of security and identity has thereby been lost. And there is no way back. Yesterday is no alternative. But to embrace Europe is to reject one's own existential basis. Nor is the way of the white man any alternative.

It is impossible for a casual white observer to have any opinion as to what may emerge from the present period of transition. Africa is an old continent, in many ways sadly worn, but possessing strong, as yet unharnessed forces. If today's crises involve a reckoning both with what is unviable in Africa's own tradition and with the patterns forced upon it by outsiders, then possibly something new may be constructed on what holds firm of the continent's own life experience. One of the elements in Africa's historical experience on which it is possible to build is the collective structure. This is what Julius Nyerere is attempting in his gospel of ujamaa villages – the Swahili word *ujamaa* can perhaps best be translated as "sense of family community". While the old villages were literally family communities, possessing an internal unity but reserved and uncooperative in their relations with the outside world, new villages are now being created with members from different clans and tribes, the sense of "family community" being replaced by neighbourliness – the basic view of common ownership and human relationships is identical in the two cases, but the new communities are expected to be more open to the outside world, more geared to collaboration with other communities. Similarly the very multiplicity of tribes that makes the nation state even more dubious points in the direction of a Pan-African consciousness, possibly with Swahili as its vehicle.

Perhaps the world will have something to learn, once again, from the experiences of Africa.

19

The peaceful vitality of the open spaces. The sense of being something that is part of oneself, beyond all conscious memory. Everything is there, as it was in the beginning. But beneath this, something else begins to ache. More and more strongly.

Sometimes people come up to our tent. They possess the simple dignity, the muted speech and self-evident grace of movement that stems from living close to a vast landscape and absorbing something of its spaciousness. You feel a soft hand in yours – lingering.

And the ache increases, the sense of sharing the white tribe's debt to the people of what we call the Third World, and which was mankind's first world.

When the tribes re-met after their long and separate wanderings, a trusting handshake would surely have been possible. As a rule, those with the darker skins greeted the whites without prejudice, openly. Since then, too much has come between them. At the Rendille's wretched waterhole a few days ago, some dry statistical data acquired eyes, lips and skin.

The space around our dwindling resources is becoming increasingly crowded. A population growth of 3 per cent per year, a rate noted in many countries, would mean that a country with a population of 15 million people today would have 285 million in a hundred years' time. In the coming century, the population of Africa would thus increase sixfold, to reach a figure of 2,300 million – which as recently as in 1940 was the entire world population.

These are impossible figures. Even so, with half of the Third World's population under the age of sixteen, a doubling of the world population by some way into the next century would seem inevitable – unless such growth is hindered by mass death from famine. The first signs of such a famine have already become evident.

And yet the most difficult problem is not presented by the growing populations of the poor countries* – as we tend unthinkingly to imagine. It stems from the technologically most advanced countries, the affluent countries.

It is not the poor countries that are the most densely populated. It is the industrialized countries, like Belgium and Holland, the United Kingdom, Germany and Japan. Africa, with its vast area, is still sparsely populated.

However, the number of people per surface unit does not tell the whole story as regards pressure of population, and resources. The picture becomes clearer if like Georg Borgström, for example, we count in "human equivalents" on the basis of the proteins that are taken directly from the land. A high proportion of the protein intake, above all in the affluent countries, reaches people indirectly via cattle – and in a beef cow 93 per cent of the protein is lost on its way from the ground to the human being. By this method of calculation, the truly overpopulated countries are the affluent countries – with a country like the United States representing 1,600 million human equivalents, a country like Sweden 65 million.

A country is overpopulated when its natural resources are insufficient to provide for its people. The affluence of the affluent countries is only made possible by a constant inflow of soya beans, palm kernels, groundnuts, fishmeal and other

* Poor countries: as a rule, rich countries that cannot avail themselves of their own natural resources. Africa is the richest country in the world in respect of natural resources, the poorest as regards its people's standard of living.

protein-rich food from the poor countries. Most of it goes to cattle, some of it to pets. World trade, which originally took shape during the era of unbridled colonialism, operates in such a way that the food goes to those who pay most, not to those who most need it. Now, as previously, starvation is business.

The white world has become an oasis of superfluous consumption on a globe in which over half the population lacks adequate food, clean water, and the materials for a decent dwelling. With today's pattern of distribution, the earth is already overpopulated. And a doubling of the population of the affluent countries would exert a five times stronger pressure on the earth's resources than a doubling in the poor countries.

We talk of "helping" the poor countries. To say that it is they who are helping us would be excessively naive. In actual fact our affluence is their distress. People who in their own banality believe in the banality of all things speak scornfully of Doomsday prophecies. Doomsday is already here for the 50 million who die each year of starvation and the diseases of under-nutrition, and for the 500 million children who fail to get what they need for their physical and mental development.

It is we who pass the sentence – to get the proteins for steaks and cutlets, broilers and lap-dogs. We let the fragile soils of other continents be laid bare to the very gravel to get our favourite crops. We let white companies encroach upon the already overworked savannahs with their cattle ranches and farms, to feed the industrialized countries. We push the poor native farmers up the mountainsides, which are close-felled to create new fields, thus causing further erosion.

Does this warm, black hand burn in yours? You have a share in the guilt, for the silent, daily tragedies played out in mis-appropriated land and in the brains of children who cannot develop naturally because they do not get enough protein. And you feel a suffocating sense of helplessness in a system that man has created, but is not capable of mastering.

Other data, too, flickered past at the waterhole.

The superpowers have stockpiled nuclear warheads enough to

annihilate each other fifty times over, and are continuing to stockpile in order to be able to annihilate each other a hundred times over. Hardly any stockpiling of food has taken place. The world spends over 100,000 million pounds a year on armaments, and less than 6,000 million on what we call foreign aid. Almost half a million of the most acute brains in the world are involved in the design of ever more diabolical weapons of destruction. How many are working on the problems of human survival?

Africa presents problems – hard, sharply delineated as the shadow on the desert sand. But its problems are the world's. Just as this part of the world is in process of drying out so, too, the whole world is rapidly declining. Where the soil is thin, and in other places where the topsoil has been torn from the ground, the damage is often irreparable. In large areas, however, it is still possible to reverse the fatal trend.

The raids made on the earth's forests *can* be stopped. Hillsides and the areas around river sources *can* often be reforested and given shade. What used to be grasslands *can* be given back their green mantle, herds of cattle *can* be reduced to what the earth can support when it is at its dryest – and the richly varied biomass of the world's wild life *can*, by sensible economic planning, replace domestic animals as a source of meat in the tropics. Arable land *can* be devoted to a variety of crops that afford protection against both heat and rainstorms. The spread of the deserts and dispersal of the soil *can* be stopped, the moisture-wasting clouds of the Sahel be dispersed and the rain perhaps be persuaded to return – insofar as the deserts, the clouds of dust and the droughts are the work of man.

All this is technically possible, and obviously, in a global perspective also economically possible – it is a question of where man's resources and intelligence should be deployed. The obstacles are of a different kind.

We have to begin, literally, at the grass-roots. That is where the catastrophe has its origin. And none of the subsidiary problems can be dealt with in isolation. What we need is a series of measures that are co-ordinated with each other and rationally incorporated in the overall ecological context.

Two disparate worlds, those of modern technology and ancient wisdom, the worlds of space and of all that is close to the grass-roots, should be able to collaborate in this task.

Space can provide one of the keys to ecological economics. From space we can see just how thin is the flesh covering the bones of the continents. Earth satellites, the main function of which has so far been to obtain military intelligence, could surely be used as ecological intelligence units, recording where the earth is in process of being laid bare or torn apart, and how the dust clouds drift towards the seas. What from the ground appears as an isolated phenomenon, can be seen in a wider context from space. It would be possible from space to sound the alarm if the earth's leprosy was threatening to spread, and to indicate where action should be taken.

The other key is provided by the small, often very small, farmers, with their insight into the terms on which one can deal with nature, an insight founded on the experience of countless generations. While modern technology is often limited in purpose, inflexible, and energy-intensive, the simple smallholder's relationship with the earth is often incorporated in an almost mystical way in a broader life context.

It should be possible for the new eyes of the Space Age, and primaeval understanding of and tenderness for the earth – the mother, the giver of life – to collaborate in solving the problems relating to the continued survival of the species.

But this presupposes that no tribe can be allowed to go on living over another tribe's means. The white tribe must give up its dominion over the world's food and raw materials, content itself with its own territory. If it does this voluntarily, there *may* still be the chance of an honest handshake over the tribal frontiers. If not, the old peoples that we call ''new'' will force us back; against their curse, no stockpiles of nuclear arms will suffice.

What we need is something of the spirit of the *kraal*, on the global scale.

The kraal is not a more or less compact agglomeration of dwellings containing people without relationships towards each other. The kraal is a unity in which all are related to each other, depend upon each other, help each other. The principle of the kraal is often the same as that which filled the white invaders with astonishment when they came storming in among the maize-growing, bean-growing Indians on the other side of the Atlantic. Each family had received by lot a piece of land to till, and was permitted to keep the fruits of his labour. Anything it thought was in excess of its own need was sent to a common store. If anyone used up his own store, he had free access to the common reserve, which could also be used to assist neighbouring villages which had had a bad harvest, or to offer supplies on the way to strangers and travellers. The unwritten law of the kraal can be classified as an insurance, a sense of solidarity based on self-interest: if I help you today, then I can expect help in return the day I find myself in trouble. The spirit of the kraal served the interests of survival.

When the spirit of the kraal was lost, some time during the migration from the Valley, an element of self-protection was lost with it.

The deserts that cover man's earlier cultures demonstrate the fragility of human civilization. One day, the desert wind can sweep in over our own oasis.

Our lack of solidarity within the species simply reflects our lack of solidarity with the earth. What other tribes have suffered is a secondary expression of the ecological rape and waste of resources that has characterized, above all, the advancement of the white tribe.

Our debt to other tribes is part of our great debt to the earth. Our debt to the earth is a debt in the present, but above all a debt to the future.

Nowhere does one experience this with such searing intensity as in the wilds.

20

Forests became deserts, lakes vanished, broad rivers dried up. But 1470 casts his shadow over the transformed landscape. His path became your path, the path of all humanity.

You came to seek a mood in man's own Valley. You are looking for a formula that holds valid and affords explanations beyond the Valley itself.

Did there exist, in the beginning, different possibilities within the brain for which the earlier primate's cranium became too small? Or was the path we have travelled the path that we were bound to go?

Evolution – as a process, a direction? Even if it operated without purpose or aim, events can be logically ordered in a causal chain leading to a situation in which the species seems to have lost control over its own growth, its own treatment of the earth, over production and distribution. But this does not mean that there did not also exist other possibilities – as yet untried.

The wilds make things simple. Their characteristic feature is immediacy. Here, everything is reduced to its basic elements. To the sun that draws the water from the oceans, and announces its fiat to the winds. To the rain, the topsoil, the grass.

It was when the curiosity and inventiveness that are the species' weapons in the struggle for survival enticed us into a host of indirectnesses that we lost our grip of the whole. The longer the road travelled, the more our sense of immediacy was weakened, and the more our feeling of not belonging increased – we became strangers to ourselves.

The species cannot renounce its curiosity and inventiveness without castrating its future. It is when these are used out of context that they can lead to the dangerous partial knowledge that confuses superficial awareness of limited facts with knowledge, and knowledge with wisdom.

In order to survive we must recover our feeling for context, our sense of immediacy – this is the interpretation of the simple message of the wilds.

Space. Stillness. Dusk slides over the savannah. Somewhere, near a thicket of acacias, an elephant lifts his trunk and sounds a tattoo to the sunset – as he did many ages ago when a creature not unlike yourself squatted by his first camp-fire. And against an eastern sky of glassy green you glimpse a misty blue shape – Kilimanjaro.

The Dream of
Kilimanjaro

I

The White Mountain – Kilima Njaro.

It captures one's glance, and holds it fast. Created by the forces of the Underworld, it affords a cool resting-place for the clouds. Its might and its stillness are overpowering. The world, it is true, houses fifteen higher peaks than this. They, however, are the culminations of great *massifs*. The grandeur of Kilimanjaro is that it rises solitary from the high plain.

Its might is strangely weightless. At a distance, the mountain can seem ethereal. When the sun is low and the clouds light, the mountain with its white-shimmering cap seems at times to be floating in space. At such moments, Kilimanjaro seems almost supernatural in its beauty.

Those living within its orbit have the mountain constantly imprinted on their retina. Its colours may shift from the orange of dawn to its characteristic tone of misty blue, deepening at times to indigo. Its cone may appear in bare outline or surrounded by monsoon clouds, which it catches and milks so that they fail to reach the plain. Its appearance may alter, but the mountain is always there.

When early man raised his eyes from the Valley, he must have been seized by dumb wonder at the blue cone towering up from the plateau. From an early stage, the mountain must have exercised a mental attraction, like the physical attraction exercised by large bodies over smaller. A brain filled with mists, like the clouds that could hide the pate of the mountain, must have pondered, vaguely, its secrets; an incipient imagination must have sought its meaning.

Slowly, wonder brightened into dreams; imagination found, as it thought, a meaning in shapes that the imagination itself created. When man, in his attempts to explain the forces of nature, began to create deities in his own image, it was natural that he should assign them an abode high up on the mountains which linked the ground on which he himself lived to the spheres in which the winds had their dwelling, the rains their origin, and the sun, moon and stars their courses.

Mountains acquired a central status in the religious concepts of different tribes. On the sister volcano to Kilimanjaro, on the other side of the equator, white-streaked Kere Nyaga (now known as Mount Kenya), the Kikuyu placed their god Ngai, who at the beginning of time had called the first man into being. People still point to the place where grew the tree from which Ngai took the first Kikuyu with him up to the snow-clad peaks and showed him the fair country below, with its woods of cedar, bamboo and olives, interspersed with open areas in which antelopes and gazelles peacefully browsed. It was there that Ngai made his covenant with the first Kikuyu: "You and your descendants shall enjoy for ever the beauty of the country, and its fruits; yet remember always that it is I who have conferred it upon you."

Of all the mountains to which the gods were drawn, few could exercise such a power of attraction as Kilimanjaro. The Massai made it their holy mountain. The Chagga, who live on the slopes once formed by fire and ash, a people who love their mountain and cannot imagine a worse fate than to move down to the drought and the heat of the plain, have their god Ruwa dwelling on the heights of Kilimanjaro – Ruwa, who like the universe has always existed, and who is the sun himself, with the moon as his wife and the stars for children. Ruwa, who created man, the beasts and all nature, is the protector of all things, the giver of all good gifts.

The reverence of the Chagga people for Kilimanjaro is focused on Kibo, its highest peak (which fortunately eluded the attempts of its first white climber to rename it Kaiser Wilhelm's Peak). Kibo incorporates all that is beautiful and invigorating. It is Kibo that causes the rain-clouds to bless the earth. When you meet someone you wish to honour, you step aside so that the other is the closer to Kibo. Anyone coming from higher up, from the direction of Kibo, will greet you first, since he comes from the quarter that brings good fortune. While the dead, in many cultures, are buried with their faces to the rising sun, the Chagga bury their dead facing Kibo. And while alive they pray, facing Kibo, their prayer to Ruwa: "Sow among us the seed of fruitfulness that we may multiply like bees; may our clan always hold together, not to be cut short in its budding, and may strangers never occupy our groves."

On the saddle between the twin peaks of Kilimanjaro, Kibo and the slightly lower Mawenzi, is a cave called Nyamba ya Muungu – the dwelling of God. It lies among wild blocks of lava, thrown out from the bowels of the earth.

There is someting symbolic about the god having been assigned his dwelling where the Underworld meets the heaven – the god who protected the clan and safeguarded its territory, but who also embodied man's dream and intimations of participation in something beyond the mountain.

2

Still your hunger, quench your thirst, carry forward the miracle of life – this trinity lends its rhythm to all life, and weaves the territorial patterns of the species. It accompanied the hominid as he imperceptibly slipped over a frontier at which he became human.

As man began to discover himself, his existence acquired a new dimension. What, in the beginning, moved, wordless in an evolving brain? You find no answer to this question as you stare into a pair of empty eye-sockets through which days and seasons once wandered, with images of valleys and mountains, forests and water. Other trails, however, carry us some of the way back towards the dawn; and where these trails stop, intuition must take over.

Embedded in the multiple ambiguities of the myths lies a message of early man's life experiences, a message that has been carried forward through countless ages and the essentials of which, at least, can be decoded.

Some of mankind's human fossils, the Stone Age tribes that have lingered into the Space Age in the isolated niches to which their ancestors once led them, and that have been so difficult of access as to escape to the last all contact with the outside world, permit us to peer into an ancient, but still vital conceptual world.

A few days' journey from our camp-site in the Inturi's forest, which constitutes the navel of Africa's physical body, above the western arc of the Rift where the sources of the Nile and the Congo meet, lives a recently "discovered" pygmy tribe, the Mbuti, who have not even learned to make fire by rubbing sticks together but who bear onwards their hearth's constantly guarded fire to new settlements and new generations. The English anthropologist Colin Turnbull, who came by coincidence to live and hunt with the tribe, has given us some glimpses into the green temple of a primitive nature worship.

The Mbuti are one with the forest. The key group is the family, but the clan is the more significant social unit, in that a life of hunting and gathering demands collaboration at all levels. The ultimate guardian of Mbuti life is the forest itself. For the Mbuti the forest is a living creature, generous if it is treated well, grudging if it is abused. Its trees and bushes provide dwellings, tools and household implements; its beasts, bees and plants provide food. When a child is born, it is wrapped in bark hammered out and softened with an elephant tusk; it is given its first bath in the sap of a tree, the forest's own water – thus it is accepted from the beginning into the community of the forest. A young hunter who has felled his first prey has his forehead marked with vertical cuts, which are filled with a paste of ashes and forest herbs – a sign that the forest is in his own body. When a pygmy feels particularly happy he may go to a glade and dance, with the forest as his partner. The pygmies sing to the forest, not in order to entreat its might but to express their harmony with the forest. At tribal ceremonies, a wooden horn is brought from its secret place high up in a tree, to be played so melodiously that the forest listens and is pleased. The forest, in its turn, gives strength to all who touch the horn, and to those who dance around the camp-fire with the horn as a phallic symbol and an expression of the life-force of the forest. Beneath these manifestations of joyful and grateful absorption into the forest, we find an extremely perceptive observation and great knowledge of the forest and its conditions – without such knowledge, the mysticism would lack depth.

What the primaeval forest has been to the pygmies, the plains and mountains, coasts and desert oases have been to other tribes: a force flowing through the ages, a force of which man himself has been part. What we can see carries us a short way down into the Stone Age. Long before that, however, intuition, man's legacy from pre-human existence, in combination with an awakening intellect that began to ask "why", must have clothed all that protected life and carried the spark of life further with a shimmer of matter-of-fact mysticism.

In materially simple communities, there is often a tremendously strong feeling for the actual place. The territory, after all, was the basis of both material and spiritual existence. The more grudging the conditions of life, the more jealously was the territory guarded. When the whites came to Australia, they noted how the aborigines grew hysterical, shouted, gesticulated, brandished weapons, burst into tears if anyone passed through their territory. Among tribes dwelling in the desert mountains between 1470's home tract and Somalia, the passing traveller should leave marked sticks as his calling-card – alien footprints betray an encroachment that must be expiated.

This sense of affinity with a small patch of the earth was a total experience. It covered everything: the ground, the plants, the animal life. Dawning religious conceptions animated everything in the surrounding nature with forces that could bring luck or ill fortune. The economic, social and religious life of the clan was interwoven with the forces and entities of nature, with which it was necessary in one's own interest to achieve harmony.

A fellowship with the beasts of the earth and the birds of the air is reflected in the accounts, contained in numerous myths, of an age of Paradise, when the animals, who know the secrets of life, spoke a language that man understood. When the shaman, in his ecstatic dance, imitates the cries of beasts and the song of the birds, he is seeking, obscurely, to recreate the state described in the Paradise myth. By entering the animal, he makes himself and the clan party to the animals' secrets and magic power. In colder climes, the process of going berserk, entering a "berserker rage", was a rite in which male youths identified with the bear.

The already animated world was entered by the clan as a whole when it sought safety and protection in a totem – which was sometimes the animal constituting the clan's staple food, the animal whose flesh and blood the clan united with its own. Man himself was the abode of a spiritual force that was in communication with the totem of the clan. In several areas we encounter the belief that this totem, after the man had had physical intercourse with the woman, entered her womb to conceive the child – a Stone-Age version of the Holy Ghost. The spiritually multi-dimensional worlds of these materially simple communities allowed for both physical and spiritual paternity.

The vital communications between the clan and its totem required ceremonies. The image of the totem became the object of cult and invocation. When young men were gradually initiated into the traditions of the clan, and the secrets of life, it was as important that they should learn the arcane rites and songs of the totem as the places where water might be found. The useful and the holy were one – everything was holy that safeguarded the continuance of life.

When man created the first gods in his own image, traces of the beast lingered. The transition can be seen with almost excessive clarity in the many-headed pantheon of Egypt. Along the banks of the Nile pass a whole procession of animal gods: from the shoulders of Thoth rises the long neck of the ibis; Horus bears the head of a hawk, Anubis that of a jackal, Khnoum that of a ram, with curved horns. Other gods bore the signs of the bull, the lion, the hippopotamus and the crocodile – the tutelary deity of Lower Egypt was the snake, that of Upper Egypt the vulture. A whole ark of animal gods has been stranded on the shores of the Nile. Many of them have come from the mountains of Ethiopia, others possibly from the savannahs and forests in the Valley and by the great lakes. Thus the early experiences and message of Africa, in the form of tribal totems, travelled down along the Nile Valley to gather as a court of national deities.

Almost unnoticeably, certain gods free themselves from their totemistic past and assume human shape. Among them was Osiris, Lord of the Cosmos, who gave man the gift of civilization, taught him to cultivate cereals and the vine, the god of life, the god of death, the god of fertility, whose erect male member the women set in motion with strings during fertility processions. Beneath his human shape we glimpse earlier forms of revelation, both as trees and beasts – it is as if the myth has intuitively captured, in the guises of the gods, that evolution for which the intellect has only thousands of years later found the theoretical evidence.

The sense of mystery, after all, seeks such embodiments as will harmonize with the contemporary surroundings and historical situation. In early society life itself was dominant, not things and their possession. The mystery of life was to be encountered everywhere in nature; everywhere, people saw fertility symbols around which a creative imagination could spin its myths. Thus the tree, whose sap was identified with the juices of both the man and the woman, could grow into the Tree of Life, the Tree of Knowledge, the cosmic tree joining earth with heaven. Thus Osiris, the god of fertility, could develop from the figure of a bull, while Zeus could re-assume the guise of a bull when he abducted and fructified Europa, the Phoenician princess who gave her name to a continent.

A symbolism of many and ambiguous meanings was attached to the snake, which was to be found both by the roots of trees and in their branches. Among the Babylonians, the serpent steals the Tree of Life; among the Hebrews, it tempts with the fruits of Knowledge; in an Indian myth, a snake with a human face picks the fruits of the Tree for man. Moses raises the serpent from the desert sand in his uplifted hands, as too does the snake-woman of Crete. It is in the form of a snake that Zeus visits Persephone, goddess of the Underworld, and begets with her the original Dionysos.

The snake was often seen as a phallic symbol – possibly because it so often dwelt by life-giving springs and bodies of water. Some tribes saw the rainbow as a huge snake filling the water-holes. On the Ivory Coast, rainmakers dance with poisonous black cobras to persuade the clouds to give their liquid to the earth. Sometimes the serpent coils around the phallic stone columns raised as fertility symbols – in the same way as it enfolds the rod of Aesculapius. In that they emerged silently and suddenly from holes in the ground, snakes were also often associated with the spirits of the dead, and were not to be killed. The snake united in itself fertility and death, two sides of the same mystery.

The same earth from which the grass grows, the trees rise, and man himself is sprung is the place to which all things return. Dead members of the clan were as the grass that withered or the leaves that fell from the branches of trees. The womb of all things was also the grave of all things, and gave them rebirth. We find even in Neanderthal man a burial custom that is still practised by several African tribes as an expression of the Life Cycle: the dead are buried curled up in the same position as a foetus in the womb.

Woman, the giver of birth, the human embodiment of the generous earth, represented the continuance of life in a very special way. At an early stage the Earth Mother and mother goddess assumed a central role in the conceptual world that centred on fertility and the renewal of life, and was perhaps the first deity to acquire entirely human shape. By the time Cybele, Artemis and Aphrodite emerge from the shadows, they have already travelled a long way. But just as life and death pre-suppose one another, so too the goddess of creation is often also the goddess of death: a goddess with two faces, one turned towards the morning, the other towards evening.

Together with her child, the mother goddess becomes the Madonna figure in which the miracle of life's renewal has found one of its most beautiful expressions. It is striking how often one finds in the churches and chapels of Southern Europe a black Virgin with a black child – for the most part relegated to some out-of-the-way corner, and replaced in the prayer niche by a white equivalent. The Madonna figure and all she stands for seems, like so much else, to be a legacy from Africa.

Gods migrated, some of them became extinct, others evolved further. Whether they took shape in an animal totem, earth spirit, or mountain god that safeguarded a group's vital territory, or in an earth and mother goddess who linked man with the ground, they embodied early man's mysterious experience of the oneness of all life.

When men lifted their eyes unto the hills, whose summits seemed to touch the stars, it occurred to them that the spark of life might have been kindled by an encounter between heaven and earth. Thus, man touched upon another new dimension, that of the cosmos.

3

In the great stillness under a tropical night sky, timeless, clear, and very close, one can be overwhelmed by a feeling of being lifted outside oneself, of becoming part of a vast calm, a security and rhythm extending beyond the stars.

I think that early man must have sensed, wordlessly, something of what I am clumsily trying to capture in words. His world, after all, was made up of winds and space, with the earth's warm skin under his naked feet and the vault of heaven above. When one sees a chimpanzee sitting absolutely still, fascinated by a sunset, one senses something of the emotions that the celestial lights must have aroused in an evolving human brain.

Man must have been struck, at an early stage, by the regularity with which the celestial bodies moved. Looking out over the Valley, he saw the angle of the sun change and the shadows move, falling longer in the morning and the evening than when the sun was overhead. From his camp in the open air, or through the entrance to his cave or brushwood hut, he could follow the metamorphoses of the moon, from a thin sickle in the evening sky to a luminous fullness that dominated the night sky and cast a mild half-light over the landscape. In these changes lay a message of time – the time of that which in itself was timeless. Gradually, he also became aware that the stars followed definite courses, and that they were ordered in clusters, which in his imagination assumed such shapes as filled the everyday life of the hunter.

The phases of the moon, and the rising and disappearance of the sun, resembled in a way the earthly cycle of birth, growth, decline, death and rebirth. The custom of greeting the rising sun as a symbol of life's return seems to have been in general use as far back as it can be traced. The moon came to be connected with the monthly cycle of women and with fertility – the Hittites called the moon Arma, the "pregnant one". The more men learned about the fires of space, the more they thought they would discover an interplay between the cosmos and life on earth.

Some 30–35,000 years ago, tough Ice-Age hunters moved from the Atlantic and Mediterranean coasts to the Siberian tundra, through the unfrozen corridor between the Arctic cap and the Alpine glaciers, crossing areas tramped by herds of mammoths and reindeer, areas where the cave-bear and the woolly rhinoceros roved to their downfall. Over this entire area the hunters left behind scraped and carved stones and bones with sequences of notches set at different angles. It was previously believed that these marks were purely decorative, or that they reflected man's propensity to fill a vacuum. However, the archaeologist and ethnologist Alexander Marshack, whose attention was drawn by chance to the regularity of these primitive signs, has compared a large number of marked bones and stones from the dusty cases of museums, and convincingly demonstrates that they are in fact early lunar calendars, in which the different sequences of lines denote the shifting phases of the moon.

To understand the man who laboriously, night after night, with his flintstone filled a piece of bone with period after period of signs denoting the phases of the moon, we must, as Marshack observes, try to forget all we know of the seven-day week, the thirty-day month, the year of 365 days, all the things for which we have names and figures. These notches on the bone or stone are an early attempt to capture the strange phenomenon we call time. We encounter here a thought process that is trying to create systems, testing the possibility of foreseeing, crossing distances in the future. At a more advanced stage we find in such lunar calendars carved animals and grasslike plants, which vary with the seasons – like the notations on the runic wands of Scandinavia.

And so the earliest attempts at astronomy retreat several tens of thousands of years beyond the observations of the Chaldaeans, the towers of the Babylonians, and the pyramids (often oriented towards the rising sun) of the Egyptians. The time-fixated notations of cereal grasses give us hints of the period presaging agriculture. The carved signs are not a written language, nor are they cyphers, but they bear witness to the same process of thought as would later take form in written languages and science.

And what we find is already so developed that it must have been based on a long preceding tradition. The fact that so many calendars have been preserved from the steppe and tundra age in Eurasia may be due to the lack of wood having made it necessary to use bone and stone. But prior to the steppe and tundra age, in places – like Africa – where there were forests, people probably used wooden sticks, which were easier to carve, but whose testimony has decayed.

The progress of the moon from new to full afforded a conveniently round unit of time. The moon, with its shifting phases, measured the quantity of days – the Egyptian moon-god Thoth, an immigrant from the mythologically fertile tracts around and beyond the sources of the Nile, bore a name which significantly enough meant "The Measurer".

The original lunar calendars embraced a varying number of lunar revolutions: seven, twelve, fifteen. As yet there was no criterion for the year. Gradually, it was observed how the moon, in its travels, emerged from different constellations – the lunar zodiac took shape, and the months could be grouped in years. The chronologies of the peoples of the Nile and the cities of Mesopotamia, and of the Hindus and Chinese, the Mayas and the Incas – underlying them all we can trace traditions based primarily on the moon. As the demand for precision increased, the sun was linked to the twelve signs of the zodiac, each covering its segment of a firmament that appears to be moving from west to east, while the sun, moon and planets seem to move in the opposite direction. From this division of the zodiac into twelve there developed the 360-degree scale that is still in use.

The signs of the zodiac are largely made up of animal shapes. The connection between the cosmic and totemistic systems of symbols is obvious. The bestial was absorbed into the celestial; the clan totems of hunters were transformed by the farmers of the Nile Valley into celestial signs. When Sirius, the Dog Star, the guardian and awakener, appeared on 19 July in the dawn sky somewhere by the source of the Nile, it presaged the annual flood; when the sun entered the constellation of Taurus, it was time to plough. The signs of the zodiac permeated people's conceptual world, became protective symbols, determined the lives of individuals and the fates of nations. As a legacy from their captivity by the Nile, the twelve tribes of Israel set the signs of the Egyptian zodiac on their standards (with the exception of Dan, which exchanged the scorpion for an eagle). Thus the celestial signs became once more the signs of clans.

At the four cardinal points of the zodiac, five thousand years ago, Taurus watched over the vernal equinox. Leo the summer solstice, Scorpio (who became an eagle) the autumnal equinox, and Aquarius the winter equinox. In varying combinations the man and the three animal figures emerge as the sun-god Horus' children who bear up the vault of heaven, become the cherubs of the Hebrews, appear in the vision of Ezekiel in Babylon, reveal themselves in the apocalyptic vision, and follow the evangelists into modern western churches, becoming, finally, pale shadows bereft of their original sap and meaning.

Those seeking parallels in the rich herbarium of ambiguities that these symbols afford have not failed to remind us that in Egypt, a thousand years before our own chronology, the birth of the sun was celebrated at midnight of the 25th December, when the sun was in the sign of Capricorn, also known as the stable; the sun-child was born in a stable. At the meridian the eastern star Sirius burned fiercely, while Virgo was rising over the eastern horizon depicted as a reaper with an ear of corn in her hand, or as the Queen of Heaven with a child in her arms: Isis with Horus. To the right of Sirius stood Orion, the great hunter, his belt adorned with three stars, also known as the Three Kings. When the sun in his course from the winter solstice passed, at Eastertime, the point of the sky at which it is crucified, as it were, on the cross formed by the ecliptic and the cosmic equator, it was in the sign of the Lamb.

From the exact observations of the early lunar calendars there grew an astronomy possessing an increasingly refined corpus of knowledge. The Great Pyramid at Giza, which took forty years to build, seems – unlike the other pyramids, which were burial chambers for the divine kings in which Osiris assumed mortal shape – to have been an observatory, and a storage depot for scientific instruments. Stonehenge in Britain, with its stones weighing up to thirty-five tons ranged in formation to face the sunrise at Midsummer, served as a vast open-air observatory forty centuries ago. Lenses of obsidian found in excavations in Nineveh explain why Babylonian clay cylinders were able to record phases of Venus that cannot be observed without optical instruments. That the earth was round was known in far-off times and in various different civilizations thousands of years before this concept rocked Europe – a Hindu scripture speaks of the earth as a "globe in emptiness'. In the third century of our own chronology, Diogenes Laërtios noted that the Egyptians had recorded 373 solar and 832 lunar eclipses, observations that would have covered a time span of ten thousand years.

The more we discover of the past, the further back in time the prologue to our civilization retreats. Possibly, the entire part of our culture that is based on a written linguistic and numerical system can be traced back to the laboriously carved lunar calendars. According to a theory launched by Dr Cyrus Gorden, our alphabet can be traced to the signs of the zodiac, supplemented by further signs for the days of the lunar month. The original alphabet contained roughly as many signs as there are days in the month. One can imagine that seafarers needed to keep an exact track of the time; the signs they made could be used both to calculate and make notes – according to this theory, the alphabet is the child of mathematics. If we had not learned to count via the phases of the moon, we would never have been able to travel to it. It was, ultimately, from the course of the moon across the firmament that we acquired matter for the long-term memory that lies in written characters, signs that man was later to regard as a gift from the gods – or from Promethean rebels against the gods.

Astronomy, the science of nocturnal stillness, contemplative solitude, and an acute vision, which someone has called a science for priests, dreamers and navigators, combined exact calculations of time and space with a deep feeling for the mystery of the great spectacle. The down-to-earth, man's mother planet, with all that maintained and propagated earthly life, was interwoven with the celestial phenomena in a cosmic totality that fulfilled man's need for an integrated experience of the whole.

A deep pondering of the miracle of the universe, a sense of participation in the overwhelming whole, this is the stuff of which religions are woven. Observation and reflection produced concepts of a cosmic force underlying the whole, a force that for the most part assumed human features. The evolving thought process had reached a stage at which it peopled the skies with personified powers. Up there among the clouds surrounding Kilimanjaro dwelt Ruwa, the sun-god whose union with the moon produced the stars. In other tribes and peoples, the Supreme Being appeared as Ngai or Osiris, Jehovah or Baal, the embodiments of a dynamic flow of thought which tried in its knowledge, myths and symbols to capture the various dimensions of reality.

When the Pharisees and scribes, the Schoolmen, mystagogues and fathers of the Church took charge of what man's enquiring fantasy had created, and froze its myths into creeds and its symbols into dogmas, much of the vital force was lost. The disguises in which an inner truth had been draped at a given period of time were assigned a value *per se*: the truth of the integrated experience was shattered, and replaced by glittering mosaics of part-truths and half-truths.

4

External and internal forces. External forces that instilled terror, and which man was unable to master. Internal forces that could also prove disturbing, but which he tried to master.

The former were not only benevolent forces, which brought rain and good hunting. They also caused the earth to quake and erupt in flames, and the thundering heavens to shoot arrows of fire. They drew a languishing heat over the land, and appeared in the roaring violence of the rainstorms.

No story has captured man's fear of these powers as well as the story of the Great Flood. It pours incessantly through the memories of peoples and tribes on all the continents. Arks with the original ancestors of mankind and a selection of living creatures on board drift ashore on Ararat or in the Himalayas. Others save both themselves and various plants and animals useful to mankind by seeking refuge in a cave, like the Persian patriarch Yina. The aborigines of Australia tell how the sea poured in and covered everything, the forests and hills alike; from the Hopi Indians comes a tale of how mountains were hurled into the water with a great splash, while the sea welled in over the land, and the world span through lifeless space and turned to ice; among the Greeks it was Poseidon who shook the earth with his trident until it was impossible to tell the land from the sea. The god up on Kilimanjaro, Ruwa of the good gifts, twice caused great waters to descend from the skies, washing away people and huts and animals, on both occasions because the rich had oppressed the poor – only the hut in which the poorest of the poor had been warned to gather was spared.

At some time in the past a catastrophe must have occurred, the memory of which has accompanied man down to the stage at which he himself is capable of burning the globe, or causing what remains of the ice caps to melt, so that the sea rises once more to drown his teeming cities. Via Plato, the words of the Egyptian priest Sonchi to the enquiring Solon reach our ears: "Your souls are young, because you have no tradition, no ancient faith or knowledge. You remember but one flood, there have been many, and there will be new destructions of humanity by different causes."

In the permafrost of Siberia and Canada, deep-frozen mammoths have been excavated, so well-preserved that dogs could eat their meat and ornaments be carved from their tusks. As recently as 1971, bulldozers operating near the River Indigirka dug up a number of mammoths with vegetable matter preserved in their stomachs, half-masticated grass on their tongues, and – in some cases – with their eyeballs intact. Carbon dating revealed that twelve thousand years had passed since these creatures had landed up in the freezer.

A catastrophe of incredible suddenness must have occurred some ten thousand years before our own chronology commences – whether because the fragile crust of the earth had buckled under the pressure of the ice, producing violent earthquakes, or because the earth had collided with some other cosmic body, which shifted its axis – it is worth recalling that as recently as in 1937 the earth avoided collision with a planetoid by a margin of five and a half hours.

Before man himself, with his ingenuity and inadequate insight into the universe, had created dangers all his own, the hazards of an unstable universe could only be ascribed to a higher power, consciously afflicting mankind. Gods were created by men's fear as much as by their dreams. The ultimate cause, however – that which called down the wrath of the gods – lay in man himself, in his egoism, in some sin against the whole. This was the *sens morale* of the Deluge. Its causality was naive, but it reflected a deep, underlying insight.

A distorted form of this same causality is to be found in the superstition that has seen various kinds of misfortune as the direct result of dark powers within man himself. Deaths and diseases, failed harvests and poor hunting, can still in many tribes – such as the Laguru in Tanzania – be ascribed to the magic of ill-minded persons. It is often the task of the clan's witch doctor to point out the guilty party; for this reason it is not the witchdoctors of other villages that members of the clan fear, but their own. If the witchdoctor lays a curse on a man, committing him to death within a given number of days, then the man who is cursed will die, since he believes in his own guilt and in the effectiveness of the curse. Sometimes the decision to point out the guilty party can be reached by the collective. Today, his punishment is usually symbolic. Previously the man pointed to knew what it meant when the collective's "execution squad" appeared or he saw its tracks outside his hut – he realized that his time had come and, therefore, it had come.

We find the same dark power of suggestion in the witch-hunts of Europe. It was enhanced, probably, by the fact that in a restricted and uniform community, where needs, fears and sources of pleasure were shared by all, everyone reacted in much the same way – conjoined as they were in the telepathy of the clan. This, however, also provided the framework for a more positive sort of suggestion. The shamans and medicine-men were often good psychologists. They were well acquainted both with the environment and with the obscure forces at work in man, and they knew how to deal with them. Numerous observers agree that the suggestive therapy of African tribes has been more successful in treating neuroses than latter-day Western psychology. The shaman often knew how to lift repressions and conflicts in the sub-conscious up to a conscious level in order to resolve them – thus anticipating Freud. In the same way, his rituals – with dances leading into a trance or other forms of collective suggestion – were often means of resolving and preventing conflicts within the collective.

In modern terms, the wisdom of the shaman could be interpreted as follows: if the individual bears within himself forces that can cause his own destruction and that of the community, then it is necessary to recognize that these forces exist – to try to suppress them is to flee from reality, from one's own past.

After the flood, some were able to flee in arks, or up to the mountains or into caves. No man can flee from his own past, or that of the species.

5

Feeling and knowing were originally one. That which was to be religion and that which would be science comprised an integrated conceptual world, born of a union between the intuition's existential experience of nature and the evolving intellect's search for contexts. A brain testing its possibilities of understanding the world, at the same time sought harmony with – and was shaken by intermittent dread of – the forces operating in that world .

Both totemism, with its comprehensible nature symbols, and the astrology that was born from watching the stars, reflected a sense and need of affinity – affinity with the territory that gave a group the very basis of its existence, and with the universe, whose vast expanses unfolded overhead. The feeling of oneness that was drummed in ritual dances to the point of trance, or experienced in still meditation under the night sky, constituted the very essence of primitive religions.

It evolved, subsequently, in the great systematized faiths: in Taoism and Buddhism, in prophetic Judaism and evangelical Christianity, in the teachings of Zarathustra and Mahomet. It is there: not as a fossil of man's primitive past, but as the kernel under different husks. The sense of affinity with a mysterious universe, inherited from long eras of pure nature worship must, ultimately, be the force which explains the grip of the great faiths on man's senses.

When, however, man moved his gods up into the sky, a process was begun which separated the terrestrial from the celestial, the natural from the supernatural. The result of this divorce was a devaluation of the nature which man had originally worshipped. However, this process was not absolute: nature, after all, was one of God's works, and could command reverence as such.

A charming picture of the cosmogony of a transitional period is to be found in Job. The god that answers Job out of the whirlwind can "thunder marvellously with His voice" so that the heart trembleth; and He "respecteth not any that are wise of heart". In the case of Job, He deals with his self-righteousness with taunting irony: "Where wast thou when I laid the foundations of the earth? declare, if thou hast understanding. . . . Or who shut up the sea with doors. . . . When I made the cloud the garment thereof, and thick darkness a swaddling band for it? . . . Where is the way where light dwelleth? and as for darkness, where is the place thereof, that thou shouldest . . . know the paths to the house thereof? Knowest thou it, because thou wast then born? . . . Canst thou bind the sweet influences of Pleiades, or loose the bands of Orion? Canst thou bring forth Mazzaroth in his season? Doth the eagle mount up at thy command and make her nest on high?"

Here, still, we find an undertone of humility towards nature. But the humility is demanded, ultimately, by the god of the sky who has created all things. This foreshadows the direction in which the process would continue. It is no longer through nature but through supernature that man obtains the norms for his actions. Creator and creation are separated; nature becomes no longer a *thou* but an *it*.

Instead of seeking fellowship in the terrestrial, the goal of life on earth comes to be renunciation of the world, a fellowship with something beyond. The flesh, which binds man to nature with all the senses, becomes an obstacle in the path to perfection. To overcome the world, man has two choices of action: to turn his back on nature, or to master it – precisely that for which the Lord of the skies taunted Job becomes in the end His commandment. The god whom man created in his own image creates man in his – infatuated by the possibilities of his brain. Man the Godmaker becomes his own worshipper.

With the duality of spirit and matter, Plato gave the Western World a philosophical basis for the worship of intellect and the soul – while the earth and man's fellow creatures were accorded a lesser dignity, and man's own body became something to conceal and castigate. Christianity, with its roots in the Hebrew myth of the Creation – "replenish the earth and subdue it" – and Greek philosophy became an expression of human self-centredness – in contrast to ancient nature worship and the wisdom of the East. Thus was born the fatal dualism that found expression in the incongruous collocation "Man *and* Nature". The justification of Nature's existence was that it served man.

Occasionally, a mild voice was raised in protest. God's little pauper from Assisi, a heretic by comparison with whom Luther seems a crude spiritual oaf, tried to overthrow the dictatorship of man over the rest of Creation. He spoke of brother Sun and sister Moon, brother Wind and sister Water, of our sister Mother Earth, and addressed in the same way the singing cricket and the falcon, and our "sweet sister Death". Against the dogma that everything in nature was subject to man, he preached an egalitarianism of the Creation, in which everything joined in glorifying its common origin.

Francis' revolt was doomed to fail. The Church disarmed him in its most refined way, by making him a saint.

The separation of feeling and knowing which in time characterized above all Western civilization became a separation of religion and science.

A theology that had detached itself from nature burned at the stake those who called into question man as the Lord of Creation, or the earth as centre of the universe. The Underworld whose forces had once helped to produce life and in whom primitive peoples saw the womb of life, became an inferno and a place of punishment.

But science, too, which in battle against the narrow concept of the universe promoted by theology tried to clarify the laws of nature, created its own dogmas, to which it was foresworn. Newton's disciples drew from his law of gravity a mechanical picture of the universe in which all phenomena could be not only explained but also foreseen on the basis of mechanically operating laws of nature. Science fostered an increasingly advanced technology. Science itself revolutionized ways of life, technology revolutionized the conditions of life. Together they created their own myths, the myths of progress and growth.

Both theology and technology are effluences of the human brain. Even if they went separate ways, they had a common starting-point in that both assumed that man could and should master nature. Both, surely, in their historical contexts were natural stages in the development of thought, and of man's inquisitively experimental inventiveness.

Every age has its framework of orientation. The maps by which an age oriented itself can never be entirely false – and never entirely true. At a given stage of development it can prove fatal if the map is given a value *per se*, if it is confused with the reality it has tried to capture in symbols – if the husk is taken for the kernel.

Is this not the stage we have reached?

This species, which has discovered so much, and forgotten so much. We make our way through the Valley, trying to look down into the past. We see a brain evolving that contains vast possibilities. We see how, in the course of its development, it creates systems of philosophy and religion which, even if they are doomed in their historical and culture-specific forms to extinction once their time has come, nonetheless stand out as natural phases in the development of enquiring thought – in the same way as different biological forms of life have succeeded each other. We see the hand, which guided by the brain manufactured the first stone tool, working the earth's life-giving topsoil so that it rises and vanishes, and working the instruments that lift man himself into flight over the globe. We see a process, a movement; we think we can trace a direction, but remain wondering as to its destination.

On the one side this skull, in which various possibilities began to dawn millions of years ago. On the other modern man, full of suspicion and bitterness towards his own work. Suspicion and bitterness towards systems of thought and belief that no longer lend him support, as he gropes in a wasteland of abandoned convictions. Suspicion and bitterness towards a technology that has created its own wastelands, and is threatening the foundation of all life.

Something tells us that our journey cannot end in this arid terrain. What do we as yet know about the human brain? What unrealized possibilities might it still contain? What new horizons can it open to man in his search?

We stand there wondering, like a climber at the foot of a mountain, whose peaks are hidden by clouds. Doubting, perhaps, the chances of reaching the top. And yet unable to ignore the dream of what prospects must open when one reaches the top and the clouds are dispelled. Feeling we must try at least to get a little way up, and then further and further up – as far as our strength will take us.

Thoughts Under an
Umbrella Acacia

I

As the sun approaches its zenith and the ground fills with its heat, life in the grasslands stands still or seeks the shade. All animal life waits for coolness and softness to return to the air, and to the earth.

The insects have disappeared; this produces a strange silence in the landscape. Whole prides of lions fall panting down among bushes and beneath trees. Black caravans of buffaloes move from the plains to the forests. Many species of antelope follow the same daily routine.

The plains and the forests are linked by the movements of the beasts in a diurnal rhythm. But there is also a seasonal rhythm in which life pulsates between the eco-systems. When the grass disappears, the forest offers a varying number of grassland creatures a means of survival. Grassland and forest function together in a finely spun network of life.

In the park savannahs, the woodland and the grassland melt into each other. The acacias are few and far between, but their broad, flat-topped crowns provide a generous shade. The acacias are the green ceiling of Africa.

With its feather-shaped leaves, its thorns, and its sweet-smelling flowers, the genus *Acacia* has evolved a whole host of varieties adapted to different soil-conditions and climates.

Their need of water varies, from the greedily guzzling rubber acacia to the drought-resistant dwarf acacia of the semi-desert. Some species shed their leaves and rest during the dry seasons; others anticipate the rain by exploding into foliage just before the wet season, others again are evergreens. The acacias are a constant reminder of life's adaptability.

My tree on the savannah is an *Acacia Tortilis spirocarpa*. In the heat of the day, I seek its company.

> Hot wind and heat
> will lick you like a flame,
> A mantle of air and a shade-giving tree
> will shelter you.

The words of the Somalian poet Maxamed Cabdulle Xasan, leader of a famous Dervish uprising at the beginning of the century, remind us that in the tropics shade can be as important for life as water.

Such is the shade provided by *Acacia Tortilis*. It unfolds its leaves and blossoms during the dry season. This blessing it can provide because its roots grope deep down in the aquiferous strata. Under its kindly vault, the signs of life return. My *Tortilis* takes part in the interplay of life in various ways. Its branches provide a peg for the ingenious nests of weaver-birds. Its flowers give nectar to the dancing bees. The incessantly searching mouths of the herbivores find its leaves. And it is prodigal with its shade.

As the drought reduces the water-holes, waves of anxiety cross the savannah. Fierce elephants drive lions from the increasingly muddy water, rhinoceroses push elephants aside, a silent but compelling signal for departure sets whole armies of gnus and zebras in motion towards remote goals. Some creatures of the grassland can suck the last distilled drops from shoots by the grass-roots; others satisfy their need of moisture with the vapours rising from heaps of elephant dung. Some make do with the scanty juice of termites. The eland, largest of the antelopes, and the impala, the most graceful, have adapted so subtly to the drought in the course of a long evolution as hardly to need water at all. What they need is shade. And that my *Tortilis* provides.

It also has other, more sophisticated gifts. Its sweet fruit-pods, rich in carbohydrates, fall to the ground without breaking. The acacia cannot propagate in its own shadow. When the grass of the savannah has become standing hay, and when the hay has been grazed down to the roots, these fruit-pods attract the eland and the impala. They pay for their shade and carbo-hydrates by planting new acacias via their droppings. This they do along their trails and at their resting-places, where the young plants encounter no competition from the returning grass. So perfect is the interplay between tree and beasts that the seed of the acacia can only germinate after passing through the intestines of a ruminant. If the acacia is felled, the eland and the impala are deprived of shade, and thus of life. If the eland and the impala are exterminated, the acacia cannot reproduce.

Several species take part in this interplay. Dead acacias are the staple diet of termites. The termites themselves cannot digest the wood, but uni-cellular protozoa in their intestines break down the cellulose and turn it into sugar. In this way the protozoa feed the termites with acacias. The hard cemented mound nests of the termites are a characteristic feature of acacia country. On abandoned mounds there often grows a star grass which, ultimately, has the acacia to thank for its existence. The star grass is much sought after by the impala, which in its turn nourishes the grass with its droppings.

As you sit under your umbrella acacia, you can capture a few bars of life's great, always unfinished symphony. Nature is not only a free-for-all struggle. It is also the co-operation of all things with each other. The struggle and the co-operation are two sides of the same theme, point and counterpoint in the great orchestration of life.

The struggle is constantly present, visible and invisible. In the competition between species. In the intraspecific battles for territory which guarantee the food supply. And, above all, billowing along the nutritional chains by which life feeds on itself.

On the savannah there is a killing that is open, quick: a broken neck, a torn jugular, a directness in everything that suggests a secret understanding between the beast of prey and its victim, an understanding that affords the victim a swift death when the hour is come.

Beneath the open struggle for life another takes place invisibly, slowly and more cruelly. Creeping, crawling parasites drill and bite their way into the beasts of the savannah, infecting muscles and intestines, eyes and noses, lungs and livers. Some place their eggs in such a way that the larvae penetrate the brain of the antelope; others swim in the blood of the baboon and the leopard, others again have their offspring travel long paths throughout the beast's tissues before they drill their way out again. The bees which hum around the acacia blooms are penetrated by tasjinid larvae, which consume the bee from within until only a shell remains. The elephant and the rhinoceros, which have little to fear from the big cats, are laid low by parasites; the cheetah is robbed of his litheness, the impala's airy leaps become heavy and stumbling.

The fight for territory, the struggle for food, the hidden workings of parasites – all these help, ultimately, to preserve the multiplicity of life, and to prevent any species from becoming so numerous as to crowd others from the common larder, a larder that consists, in the final analysis, of the world's limited store of topsoil. Competition and death serve to maintain the balance of life. The other component is co-operation.

Competition and co-operation follow the baton of the same powerful conductor. If we have to give him a name we can call him Self-interest – the interest in carrying forward the genes of one's own species, and ultimately of the individual. In a way, the life force itself becomes identical with self-interest. So strong can be the drive to carry on the individual variant of the vital spark that a lion taking over a lioness may start by killing the cub she already has; in the same situation, some male birds can start by throwing out the eggs the hen has had by an earlier cock.

From self-interest spring family solidarity, group solidarity, the solidarity of the species. A family of elephants on the move: the older beasts form a ring around the vulnerable young, to protect them. A flock of baboons in flight: the older males cover the retreat of the females and young, and in such a situation can gang up to attack a lion or a leopard; some individuals may fall victim, but the big cat is defeated. In certain species of birds, all individuals in a given area can combine to attack any creature that is threatening a fledgling. Often, we find a co-operation across the boundaries of the species: the heron parked on the back of the rhinoceros frees the host animal from insects, and in this way obtains food and protection; when a zebra, in the manner of equids, needs to roll in the dust, a kongoni antelope can stand guard against beast of prey.

Which brings us back to the acacia – the antelope – the protozoon – the termite – the star grass. Everywhere in nature, relationships merge into each other, symbioses link and interlock. In this way, all life is toned together in an integrated whole of dependencies, impulses, symbioses. It is thus utterly meaningless to grade different forms of life into "higher" and "lower". The differences between species lie not in their quality but in their function.

No creature can exist in a sealed room. The different species presuppose each other, they meet and dictate each others' terms of life. It is sheer narrowmindedness in our species to see certain flowers as weeds, certain creatures as vermin.

The beauty and strength of life lie in the harmony of its functions. Ultimately, self-interest must lead to a sense of solidarity with all else in creation – a solidarity with life itself. Self-interest is the basis of all morality. Ecological morality entails moderation and restrictions in the struggle for survival.

If a given creature emerges all too triumphant from the

struggle for survival, if it overplays its role, then something in the fragile web of dependencies, conditions and impulses is damaged. If every form of life has its function in the interplay, then life itself becomes poorer when a given form is crowded out and the diversity reduced. Forms of life that have disappeared can never be replaced. A lost instrument is a loss to the entire orchestra, and reduces the symphony's fullness of tone. The contemporary generation may not notice it, but the future can suffer. An earth in which the richness of the species is diminishing loses something of the dynamic stability that ensures adaptation and survival.

A species that triumphs in such a way as to impair the diversity of life is a threat to its own existence. The fragility of nature can turn such a triumph into self-annihilation.

If you lack the understanding to comply with the pattern of the acacia and the antelope, then you have failed to understand yourself. The door to the green room of your soul has jammed shut.

A descendant of 1470, returned to his domain, torn between a sense of participation and a sense of alienation, seeking an identity. . . . Over the course of a long evolution you have shared the past with countless forms of life. You have no future that you will not share with others. It is in the participation, your relationships with these that you must seek your identity.

2

The ur-cell, the primate in the forests of Gondwana, 1470, you yourself – a context back towards remoteness that can only be guessed at, and at the same time a context in the present: immediate, direct, and time-erasing.

The fact that man, in his retorts, is beginning to produce some of the twenty amino-acids and other chemical components that make up life, confirms that life could have been awakened by an interplay between the original atmosphere and the primaeval ocean. The horizon of life is also being pushed further and further back. A few years ago there were found in South Africa fossilized micro-organisms resembling algae which proved to be 3,400 million years old. They contained the same complicated chemical factories as are to be found in men – which means that life itself must have begun long before that time.

Also, a succession of chemical compounds – including water – have been found in clouds of cosmic particles, compounds that must have been formed in the austere conditions of space. The missing link in the chemistry of space, the long searched-for molecule of carbon and hydrogen known as the CH radical, was recently discovered by the Swedish research worker Olof Rydbeck. Eighteen amino-acids were discovered in a meteorite that fell a couple of years ago in Australia, and which was found to be of the same age as the earth. The proof that they had been formed in space was as simple as it was convincing: while the amino-acids of the rotating earth are all ''left-handed'', those in the meteorite were mirror images of each other, some being ''left-handed'', others ''right-handed''. We begin to sense that the chemical preparations for the first earthly cell may have begun in space.

This ur-cell, which was to take form in the most varied manifestations of life. . . . Becoming the grass that moved in over the continents, the beasts that fed off the grass, the men who fed on both the plants and beasts. Becoming brains and eye-balls, tongues and intestines. Thousands of billions of cells together form a human body, with its tissues and fluids. Each cell lives its own independent life, each organism is dependent for its existence on the co-operation of independent cells. And no cell can be isolated in time. It bears an inheritance from the ur-cell, which was prepared in space.

That which we call life pendulates between stability and instability. The variegated expressions of life reflect one of the vectors of evolution; that of renewal, the search for form, adaptation. The other is to be found in persistency, endurability. The waves of the primaeval ocean still surge in every individual cell. But our ties with our origins are more direct than this. In a sense we are not ''descended'' at all. In a sense we are still in the primaeval ocean.

Each cell comprises in itself an eco-system with series of dependencies. In the miniature oceans of the cells, with their salt from the primaeval sea, swim small unicellular creatures with structures reminiscent of the blue-green algae to be found in the smallest drop of moisture on this globe. If any form of animal life is to be designated the ''most important'', then it may be these tiny creatures. They are the necessary condition of all more composite life.

The invisible lodgers in these cells – we call them mito-chondria in the case of animal life – were to be found in the primaeval ocean, where sometime in the dawn of creation they were caught or allowed themselves to be encapsulated by the ur-cell and its descendants. They have accompanied the cells all the way from the original sea, stable, unchanging, the same today as they were thousands of millions of years ago. In sperms and ova they are carried incessantly to new generations and new forms of life.

Without the mitochondria, the cells could not breathe. At the same time, the mitochondria have so adapted to the eco-system of the cell that they cannot live outside it. Their first meeting was perhaps the most primary form of symbiosis, the first note struck in life's great symphony of dependencies and possibilities. From this original symbiosis, dependence has developed to a stage at which the mitochondria are by way of being specialized organs – both for the individual cell and for the organisms that the cells co-operate to create. It is through your mitochondria that you exist. They catch oxygen for you, provide you with the energy that sets you off to hunt for food and busily to improve the world, they feel the feelings you call your own, they move your muscles, give birth to your thoughts.

The mitochondria are the frame around which evolution kneads different expressions of life. They are the constancy around which all inconstancies are formed. From the perspective of the mitochondria – which can be as valid as man's – each organism is a dwelling, a society they have built for themselves in the same way as the termites build their nests. It has been calculated that almost half of a human being's dry substance consists of mitochondria. Man, who seeks his identity, is a collection of small ur-creatures on the move. As you wander over the savannah it is a philosophical question as much as a biological one whether you are taking a walk with your mitochondria or they are taking a walk with you.

The blue-green algae that entered the plants of the primaeval ocean we call chloroplasts. Without them, the tree that gives you shade would not be there. It is through the chloroplasts that the grass and the acacias live. It is in them that the chlorophyll-green miracle unfolds, it is they that by photosynthesis brew together sunlight, water and carbon dioxide into the nutrition which causes the trees and the grass to grow. They are intermediaries in the interplay between the gases of the air and the acids and salts of the earth that clothe the continents in green. By both the vegetable nutrition they produce and the oxygen they exhale – and the mitochondria then inhale – they create the necessary conditions for animal life.

In the leaf-green ceiling above you, billions and billions of chloroplasts are at work, silent, invisible, and unfailing. They produce oxygen which you can breathe, and water vapour to soften the evening air. Food, oxygen, water vapour – and this blessed shade! You live through the ur-creatures of the plants as much as through your own.

It is at the level of the microbes that the deep cello tones in life's symphony are played, although we can only follow the melody in parts. We share enzymes with everything around us. Viruses travel freely between oceans, plants, insects and people; they seem to be a sort of migrant gene contributing to the mutations of species. The mitochondria swimming in your cells are to be found in all animal life. Through them, you are united with all creatures that have gone before, all those existing in the relative present, and all those who will fill the future, as long as life on Earth continues.

Between the mitochondria and the chloroplasts there is a constant dialogue, an antiphony between the two main forms of life. In the beginning they were presumably one, before they specialized for their roles in the great symbiosis between vegetable and animal that sets beating the pulses of life itself.

Deeper down is something more elusive. What we have brought to light about mitochondria and chloroplasts points to a oneness in all life that is as strong as the drive towards variety. This oneness is perhaps manifested in forms and at levels that we as yet can only vaguely sense.

3

A conversation! Am I conversing in a way with my acacia? Wordlessly, in a language that exists only as a sensed rhythm.

I have sometimes experienced the same thing in the great forests of the north. Then the pines, now an acacia on the savannah. In both cases an all-pervading sense of calm and well-being, beyond all the second hands and time-tables.

Times when the sense of participation is greater than the sense of being outside. But of course. My mitochondria and the chloroplasts of the trees are engaged in lively and amicable dialogue. Possibly I sense, below the level of consciousness, something of this dialogue. But it may also be a question of more subtle paths of communication.

We, after all, are constructed like the plants of the earth's basic elements. The plants represent primary life, animals and people, a secondary kind of life. Our bodies grow from the ground via grasses and leaves and the fruits of plants.

In animal life, the chemical elements have combined to form nerve systems that can feel, see and hear, capture tastes and smells. Through our nerve fibres we constantly receive information from our surroundings. If we experience well-being, anguish or pain, it is because of what our nerve fibres have picked up.

It is, surely, our notorious arrogance that has led us to believe that the chemical elements do not gather into some form of sense organ also in primary life. Watch the climbing plant groping towards its support, see the root fibres that seem to taste the earth and find the secret places where there is water, the blades and branches competing for the gases of the air – plants must have some means of communication with the world around them. Not through senses analogous to our own, but perhaps through organs of perception capable of capturing events and recording phenomena that lie to some extent beyond the range of our conscious senses.

Since all life has the same origin, there may lie at bottom a primary capacity for perception which has been inherited from life's first hesitant beginnings and continues silently to operate in all life.

One of the great scientific discoveries of our century, one that has broadened our horizon, is that all living things, from the simplest forms of life to the most composite, plants and animals alike, live in a radioactive field that can be measured with sensitive electronic instruments and recorded in graphic curves. Professor Harold Burr of Yale University, and his co-workers, who helped develop a technique by which it is possible to measure the electromagnetic radiation of different biological systems with great precision, speak of this field as the ''life-field''. In a succession of experiments, they claim to have found that the pattern of radiation altered according to different factors in the immediate environment, faithfully reflecting a person's physical and mental state. A wound, however small, or a temporary feeling of depression gave a reading on the volt-meter, and changes in the field of force could be measured at a distance of several metres from the generative source. According to Burr's theory, the life-field is both a consequence of the life process and something governing that process – we may in other words be approaching here something in the basic structure of life itself.

Numerous other reports, as yet less certain, have appeared in recent years from the same area of enquiry. The Russian brothers Kirlian, claim to have taken photographs of the life-field, using a hypersensitive electronic technique; the field is said to be so intense that if you cut a strip from a healthy leaf, the pattern of radiation still follows for a short while the shape of the entire leaf. The American criminologist Cleve Backster and others following in his tracks have attracted a certain amount of attention by experiments in which a detector has been wired to a plant and a polygraph has recorded its reactions in different situations. The findings reported by the Backster team cover three phases. The first thing they claim to demonstrate is that if a plant is injured or killed, the recording pen describes violent curves resembling those of a human being in pain and terror – which, of course, is not to say that the plant experiences pain in the human sense. The next step demonstrates that plants react to other life in their vicinity, being disturbed if other biological systems are in pain or die, and reacting positively to *inter alia* sexual activities. The final phase claims that plants react to people's thoughts and intentions: the very intention to harm a plant can give a reading "as of anguish", while people with green fingers can get plants to enjoy themselves. Indian experiments, controlled by Julian Huxley, are reported to suggest that plants can be activated by music: while noise produces negative reactions, quiet music from, say, a violin and flute could stimulate growth, flowering and fertilization.

As yet we should perhaps maintain a critical distance vis-à-vis the "Kirlian effect" and the "Backster effect". Their scientific foundation is as yet fragile, and in so new a field of observation it is easy to stray into occultism.

An attitude of critical caution, however, does not imply blind rejection. Only three hundred years ago the observation that plants have a sex-life was dismissed as "the wildest fancy ever to have sprung to a poet's mind". Our established concepts are subject to a law of inertia. The model we construct of the reality we think we see, is delimited both by the coarseness of our senses and the bounds of our imagination. Far too often we find only what we expect to find. We protect our model in time, reject anything that upsets us – which means anything that threatens to disrupt the prevailing picture of the world.

The history of the natural sciences should have taught us never to exclude the possibility of the seemingly impossible. In the case of life's silent means of communication, we have before us what is assuredly a rewarding field of research. Even if the earliest pathfinders prove to have strayed somewhat from the track, we may take it for granted that we will discover senses in ourselves and in our fellow creatures that will revise our concepts of how life is structured. With further research, phenomena that previous generations regarded as supernatural may acquire explanations as natural as they are fascinating.

Telepathy and other parapsychic phenomena that were not previously considered suitable guests in the clinically cool atmosphere of a laboratory are now the subject of serious research. Researchers are no longer seeking evidence of inter-personal communications beyond the vocal language and visible signs: instead, they are investigating how such communications work. We begin to glimpse beneath the thresholds of the everyday self parapsychic contexts through which we are in continuous contact with a reality invisible to our ordinary senses.

Researchers may be on the track of something similar in the case of plants. Plants breathe, without possessing gills or lungs. They digest food, without stomachs. They move without muscles. No mystification need be involved if they can also perceive, without possessing the nervous system peculiar to animal life.

The key to what we see may lie in the electromagnetic fields, and in the observation that these function even in and around the individual cell. Every living thing is built up of cells. If all life is organized and controlled by a field of force operating at the cellular level, then it is no unreasonable thought that the individual cells contain primary organs of perception that put them in communication with all other life. In which case they would be the self-evident intermediaries between the two main forms of life, between the animal and the vegetable life-systems.

We do not know what electromagnetic fields consist of. It has been hazarded that they stem from vibrations in the plasma, thinner than a whisper, that fills 99.99 per cent of the universe, forming a fourth element in addition to the solid, the liquid and the gaseous. What we do know is that an electric field can be influenced by another electric field. When the waves from two life-fields meet, some form of dialogue must surely take place.

In the muddy rivers of Africa live small electric fish that investigate their surroundings with their fields of radiation and register when a suitable prey comes within range. An English biologist has suggested that a human being, with his weaker field, scans his surroundings in much the same way to register in a manner that we term intuitive the thoughts and intentions of other members of the species – an ability that seems to be more marked among peoples living close to nature than in those we call civilized. Such scanning processes may be the sixth sense by which the impala perceives the intentions of the wild dogs. If all life emits waves and is sensitive to waves, then we may have a possible theoretical explanation why plants appear to be able to react to the pain, pleasure and intentions of other creatures.

We have now an intimation that our journeys of discovery are bringing us close to worlds beyond the visible world registered by the inadequate senses of our daily self. We may be in process of discovering a dimension beyond the three-dimensional world that physics has so far described – a dimension of which the three-dimensional world may be only a shadow.

In a way we are discovering nothing new. The pygmy who sang for the forest, the Indian who asked the tree to understand why he had to fell it, had in their way a truer knowledge of the tree than the cellulose experts of our own day. What may now happen is that we, with the help of complicated instruments created by the intellect, confirm what the people we call primitive knew intuitively. If we succeed in following the trail far enough back, we may arrive at the primary capacity for perception and communication that existed before life divided itself.

Perhaps it is our forgotten mother tongue we are rediscovering. My conversation with the acacia may be supremely real. If it gives me the same timeless sense of oneness as can be experienced under a starlit night sky, it is no coincidence. The force that binds together the different forms of life must utlimately be a cosmic force.

4

As we grope towards another reality, a new dimension, as elusive yet as a desert mirage, as unclear as the prospect from a cloud-swept mountain, our habitual concepts and formulae lose their meaning. Such concepts as organic and inorganic matter and elementary particles are verbal illusions that we have carried with us from an earlier picture of the world.

Juat as there are strong currents connecting animal and vegetable life so, too, the boundary between the organic and inorganic forms of what we call matter appears to be a fiction. The same elements – those we call elementary particles – form the atoms in mountains and men, in galaxies and mitochondria. The possibilities of life are contained in inorganic matter.

Increasingly, matter itself is beginning to emerge as something immaterial. The elementary particles no longer seem to be either elementary or particles.

At the level of the atoms, where electrons dance around the nucleus at the same relative distance as the earth around the sun, a vacuum pre-dominates – but a vacuum in which there are forces at work holding the atoms together, just as invisible gravitational forces tie together the planetary systems. Just as the atom, so long indivisible, has allowed itself to be divided into electrons and protons, so too we begin to realize that what we have taken to be elementary particles may be made up of still smaller elements. Need there, indeed, be any "smallest unit" in that which forms the worlds observed by our senses? The idea that one can split up the building bricks of the universe until one arrives at something that can no longer be split stems, surely, from the fact that our delimiting concepts of space tempt us to think in terms of limits to size, both largeness and smallness. Just as the universe, the macrocosmic largeness, must be assumed to have no limit in space, so also there may be no limits downwards and inwards to the microcosmic smallness – nothing constituting an ultimate foundation.

Nor are what we call particles properly speaking particles, they are something that behaves in a certain way. When we now say we know of some fifty elementary particles and as many anti-particles, we are speaking of the properties of an atom with which we consider ourselves familiar. What we have found so far, which is as confusing as it is helpful, cannot be "ultimate". We can glimpse properties underlying properties underlying properties – *ad infinitum*. Beneath the variety may lie sources of energy that we are today unable to imagine.

What man thinks he is discovering as he peers into the micro-worlds of Creation is difficult to capture in a language built on entirely different premises. The property that man, in his enquiry, now observes can perhaps be described as vibrations (although we do not know what is vibrating). In such a description the entire cosmos emerges as a vast scale of vibrations. Waves and particles are simply different names for the same thing. The atom consists of the radiation it emits. Matter becomes identical with energy. Man becomes a creature of vacuum, consisting of properties held together by electro-magnetic and nuclear forces, which extend moreover beyond the body visible to the human eye.

Somewhere in this play of properties and forces is your identity as a species and as an individual – the identity of your participation. Drowned in your age, the prisoner of its concepts, you can glimpse only the direction in which you should seek it.

The compass points to the cosmos. The properties that formed our planetary system were swept together from the vast wastes of the cosmos, and will return whence they come when the system's central body one day erupts in a gasping nova. A human "I" draws breath in a fluttering second of eternity as it passes, but the properties which formed that "I" have never left eternity.

It is from the central body, a sun whose weight is equivalent to that of three hundred and thirty thousand earths, that the primary conditions permitting life on earth proceed. The energy that at a temperature of many million degrees is generated in the nuclear reactor inside the sun makes possible the shadow of the tree, and your own fumbling thoughts. Its rays would bounce against a burned-out globe, had they not to pass through the sun's dense plasma, the compact vacuum-suspending mass of free electrons that slows down the waves as they pass, and dims their light: it takes, apparently, twenty thousand years before they reach the surface of the sun from its nucleus – eight minutes later they reach the earth. The light just now flooding the savannah was generated in the Stone Age and the Ice Age.

The sun not only causes light and heat to shimmer over the landscape, where it produces each second more energy than man has liberated since 1470 rose from his valley. Each second it hurls out some ten thousand million tons of atomic nuclei and electrons with the solar wind. The small fraction that reaches Earth is sufficient to influence life on the planet.

Also, millions of tons of meteoric dust rain down from space every year. Your flesh is built of matter that aeons ago was swept in from the cosmos, and of cosmic matter that is reaching you here and now. Matter also travels from earth into space. Planetary systems seem to suck matter from each other – in a sort of cosmic metabolism that affects our own metabolism. Without the exchange of cosmic matter, we would not be what we are.

One of the particles or properties that reaches us from space is the recently discovered neutrino, the main property of which is to have none – no mass, no electric charge, only vibrations. Generated in the sun, it passes the massive wall of the solar electrons in a second, sweeps through the earth as if it were not there, streams in its billions through your brain while you pronounce its name. From the perspective of the neutrino, the sun may appear as a mist and the earth with its life as a vacuum – and there is no reason why the neutrino's picture of the world should be any less true than ours. Yet it must have some task to perform in the vacuum, something that can have an important bearing on what we call life.

We live in a way in an illusory world, in that our coarsely grained senses can only register fragments of our environment. The eye, which sees, took shape in darkness. The ear, which receives the waves of the air, emerged in outline in the waves of the ocean. The nerves with which we feel began as an irritability in the early protoplasm. The eye, the ear, and the sensory nerves only capture the aspects of nature that we must receive in order to fulfil our biological role in the interplay. They interpret messages and signals for our own purposes.

But with finer, more pristine and concealed sentient organs we are also at every moment the receivers of messages and influences from cosmic sources, partakers in silent but vital conversations. If life is electromagnetic vibrations, then it must be in a constant dialogue with other electromagnetic vibrations. In actual fact, the brain and the central nervous system, the delicate products of evolution, appear to be extremely sensitive receivers for the vibrations that fill nature – indeed, which are nature.

Around us are forces that we can only glimpse but which are so fundamental to life that they can be said to be part of life. The most immediate are the earth's own magnetic fields. We do not know how they are generated. An attractive theory is that the fluid core of the earth rotates faster than its crust, which is slowed down by the friction of the tides. Our spinning globe, with its different speeds as between the core and the crust, thus acts as a dynamo, producing the electromagnetic fields which surround us.

These fields, however, alter with the positions of the sun and the phases of the moon. They thus determine the rhythm of life. Algae and salamanders shut up in sealed containers have shown themselves to be mysteriously aware of the waxing and waning of the moon. Embryos that have never seen the celestial bodies have been found to have a sort of genetic knowledge of their paths. Professor Frank Brown, who has studied these phenomena in detail, believes that such organisms have their own compass needles which react to the magnetic fields as they vary according to the juxtapositions of the sun and the moon to the earth.

When sun-spots or solar eruptions occur or when magnetic storms tear across the sun's surface, it affects not only the earth's magnetic field but also the weather and the winds, and the blood serum and moods of living creatures. The way in which occurrences of sun-spots are grouped in eleven-year cycles, within even larger-scale cycles, is reflected, for example, in the annular rings of trees, in records going back several thousand years of the level of the Nile, and in layers of sediment that sink back five hundred million years into time. Just as all earthly life is adapted to the earth's rotation by a diurnal rhythm, and to its position in space by an annual rhythm, so too it must follow these larger rhythms.

The tidal force of the moon operates both visibly and invisibly. It dictates the pulse of the earth. So strong is the grip of the moon on the oceans that it may be something of an optical illusion to see the sea rolling towards the continents; it may rather be the rotating continents that clash against the sea. Every drop of water in the ocean is affected by the force of the moon. The smallest water-hole is affected in the same way as the ocean. It must surely also be the case that the miniature oceans in our cells move in tidal waves according to the movements of the moon – as they did when they were still part of the primaeval ocean.

Our journey, however, carries us out over still deeper waters. All life-processes take place in water, even in the organisms that have chosen the continents as their domicile. Water is the liquid of life. With nervous rapidity it changes its structure, being more sensitive than any other element to changes in electric, magnetic and gravitational fields. Water, with its rare physical properties, can be a vital medium for the communication of organisms with their surroundings; according to Piccardi, the founder of cosmic chemistry, it is something that permanently links us with cosmic forces.

The sun and the moon are neighbouring powers, around which the dawning thoughts of early man revolved. As we hurl through space on our terrestrial craft, we are also continuously exposed to forces operating over vast distances in the cosmos. The spaces between the stars are not the empty holes that it was for a while thought, once the theory of the magical substance known as ether had been abandoned. The galaxies float like archipelagoes in an ocean of plasma and the sea of space is filled with waves – from waves longer than the diameter of the earth to waves so short that a thousand million would find room on your eyeball. Together, these different vibrations constitute a great symphony of the spheres.

We ourselves are strung to their key. It was from wave sequences of this kind that life on this splintered fragment of space was once orchestrated. Other suns than ours, forces operating over a distance of light-years, worlds exploding in the spasms of novas, sources of radiation that we have only recently discovered and which defy the laws of space we have so far formulated – all these affect at every moment the earth and all life upon it.

The vibrations of the cosmos encounter your life-field – a life-field originating from the cosmos. Waves meet and an interplay occurs mutually between the organisms of earth, and between them and forces in the cosmos. Every last particle of life exists only as a part of this interplay.

Life and death have a common source – what *we* call life, what *we* call death. The rays that kindled life at the dawn of creation would also extinguish it, if they were not damped and filtered.

Life, that fragile phenomenon, must be protected by a series of shields for the rays of life not to become death-rays. While the cell's processes merge with those of its surroundings, the cell has its membrane to protect its vulnerable interior. Specialized cells build skins and membranes and shells around animals, leaves and fruits. The earth itself is veiled by the atmosphere, to the creation of which all living things contribute: in the outer layer the ozone, the three-atom oxygen, affords a protective mask against the searing breath of the sun.

Now that space ships have broken through the electric walls of space, we know that the earth is also surrounded by spherical magnetic fields that brake the solar wind, so that it reaches us only as a light breeze. But the solar wind itself seems to constitute an atmosphere that embraces the entire planetary system, creating an environment without which no life could exist in this part of space. Somewhere beyond Pluto, where the solar wind is assumed to collide with the plasma of space, there occur, according to one theory, magnetic storms, which in their turn form a gigantic bubble around the whole solar system, thus damping the intensity of the radiation from outer space.

Life can only exist beneath a series of invisible spheres providing a friendly shade, like a tree on the sun-drenched savannah.

Now, however, nature's finely tuned play of vibrations is blended with waves emitted by human technology. Silently, almost unnoticeably, man once emerged in the Valley. Things got noisier later on – until the atoms of silence were burst with a mighty bang.

Even what we regard as inorganic matter is susceptible to manmade waves. By means of a single pick-up, "dead" things have been made to speak: a clay pot to reproduce the clatter of the potter's wheel when it was formed, a painting to reproduce snatches of music played while the brush was moving in the paint. How much more sensitive must not the brain and central nervous system be to the unnatural vibrations with which we fill nature.

The foetus banging on the mother's abdomen when it hears a noise, plants that react in a seemingly pained way to disharmony, bear witness to acoustic assaults against which the individual is defenceless: since while the eye can close to what it will not see, the ear cannot close to what the body will not hear. Warning voices are trying to force the noise barrier but have difficulty making themselves heard, voices wanting us to realize that noise, both audible and inaudible, infrasounds below the audible level and ultrasounds above that level, can cause physical and mental injury, and in extreme cases shorten life.

Noise constitutes only a part of the vibrations generated by human technology, vibrations that for the most part lack the rhythms of the natural wave systems. We know very little about how organisms are affected by the radio and radar waves with which we fill the interspace between the earth and the ionosphere. Alert brains in arms laboratories are working on the idea of high-intensity waves on the frequencies of the human brain which would strike the brain itself with panic: the brain working out its own destruction – a sublime example of the morbidity of our concerns. By imitating the processes of the sun, we can also unleash a radiation against which nature's own shields otherwise protect us.

It thus seems only natural and consistent that we should be running the risk, with the nitrous oxides from our atomic tests, of tearing to pieces the thin sheath of ozone that for aeons has protected life from overdoses of the sun's untra-violet rays. Every time propellant gas is pressed from a spray container, the threat is slightly increased – a reminder that insignificant causes, when added to each other, can have fatal consequences.

We are groping forward in the first pale light over a new and breathtaking journey of discovery. A space opens, filled with glimpsed and unknown forces, and, certainly, forces beyond our present powers of comprehension.

We begin to see ourselves as instruments that with great sensitivity react alike to the movements of the galaxies and to the noise of traffic, to variations in the magnetic fields and to the life-fields of our fellow-creatures, to light, to rhythms, and to the swell of the tides in the body's own cells. We are in process of discovering that occurrences elsewhere in the cosmos intervene in our environment and in ourselves more radically than any previous mythologies imagined. We are catching glimpses of a cosmic totality, all parts of which are in relation to each other.

The great vault of space opens above us, as we crawl around on our grain of dust. It is nothing we can use, nothing we can command. It is there. And it commands us.

5

What the astronauts have discovered for us is primarily the earth: a misty, blue-shimmering body in black space, breathtakingly different from the barren lunar and Martian landscapes that we have also come to know.

From space, the earth with its delicate beauty appears as a living organism, the different parts of which co-operate like the cells of a body. Oceans and land surfaces, the atmosphere and the gauze-thin membrane of life covering the rocky skeleton of the earth, all these emerge in the perspective of space as a coherent system. Pictures from space have suddenly presented, with simple lucidity, what had been so laboriously reached by thought. It is above all the atmosphere that lends pictures of the earth their softness, lustre and movement. It is through the atmosphere that the earth breathes in space. Generated by gases from the earth's rocks, it is maintained by life-systems, at the same time as it in its turn maintains life – just as life creates the topsoil that nurtures it.

Together, the rocks, the sea, the atmosphere and life itself make up an environment that secures the conditions necessary for life. In interplay with each other they generate the temperature, the humidity, the salt content and the acidity that life demands, and part of the membrane that damps the radiation from space. They are as interdependent as the muscles, bones, blood and nerves of a body.

And so, our explorers in space – whether they themselves are physically hurled out in a capsule or journey over the light-years by means of giant telescopes – bring us back to Gaia. Gaia was the earth mother of Hellenic mythology, born of the sea, the mother of Chronos – Time – the ruler of the Gods in the Golden Age, when the earth without labour rendered man an abundance of all things. In the art of classical antiquity, Gaia raises her broad bosom from the ground; this depicts her oneness with the earth. Gaia embodied the pristine concept of the earth as the womb of all life; at the same time, we sense under the thin mythological veil the contours of the natural philosophy shaped by Thales and the Ionian thinkers who turned their gaze towards the universe, rejected the gods, and regarded matter as life itself. A modern natural philosopher – Jim Lovelock, known for his research on the atmosphere and the first to draw attention to the risks that propellant gases presented to the ozone – has chosen Gaia as the designation of an hypothesis which deepens vision of the earth as one great organism. The Gaia hypothesis assumes that the atmospheric membrane which gave the opportunity of life is not a once-and-for-all creation of the earth's rocks but something continuously held in equilibrium by the biological processes taking place on the surface of the earth. Faced by cosmic threats to its existence, matter does not remain passive. Life has developed its own defence mechanisms to keep the composition, temperature, humidity, pH and salt content of the atmosphere within the bounds that will permit life. In this way, life secures its own survival.

This is a fascinating vision, which leads our thoughts to the mysteriously self-curative forces of individual organisms. If your body is harmed, a series of protective mechanisms comes into play: your blood pressure falls to reduce the haemorrhage, the spleen sends new blood from its reserve supply, the capillaries around the wound dilate to release white blood corpuscles that can form a shield against bacteria from the outside world. The surrounding tissues release cells, which move in over the injury and form new tissue. It is as if there existed in the organism an innate pattern which strives to maintain itself. Is this also true of the organism that is the earth?

As yet, the Gaia hypothesis is an unproven line of thought. Like so many other hypotheses, it may open up paths in other directions than those originally sought. It helps us to formulate questions relating to the role of man in the Tellurian interplay.

A little way away from my place in the shade a termite mound rises up to the height of a man; in the perspective of the termite a skyscraper, higher than anything built by man. It is a monument not only to dead acacias, but also to the joint strength of a collective society. This edifice, which can house a million or so termites, is a complicated construction, with galleries and chambers and ventilation shafts that afford eggs and larvae the right temperature and humidity for survival.

If only a few termites are brought together, they rush aimlessly around each other, grope listlessly for sticks and pieces of grit only to drop them. When they are sufficiently many, it is as if a bugle had sounded, a thought had been conceived, a plan had become evident. Suddenly walls and columns begin to go up, vaults and chambers are constructed and joined, each individual act is incorporated in a meaningful whole. There appears to be no architect, no construction manager. Yet all know their task. The explanation that these tiny builders are genetically programmed for this collective enterprise takes us only half-way. It says nothing of the coherent force that has turned these blind, weak, vulnerable creatures, sensitive to the sunlight and to the slightest change in humidity and temperature, and thus apparently very ill adapted to life on earth, into one of the most successful species on this planet. To the onlooker, it seems as if their extremely rudimentary brains were combined into a collective brainpower, just as the cells co-operate in an individual brain.

Possibly, our own works and days in a somewhat larger

perspective are not greatly different from those of the termites. We may be genetically programmed to build an edifice that no individual can grasp, any more than the termite can be conceived as having any overall picture of the collective work to which he contributes. After all, our mental edifices are the works of a collective brainpower – whether they materialize as the Babylonian towers or as visions rising much higher above the surface of the earth. Civilizations that have come and gone, based on the same realistic grounds as biological evolution and decaying when they betray the foundation that supports them, have been collective achievements, with their columns and arches, as much as the termite mounds. Our aggregate wisdom is composed of knowledge from different places and ages – and its collective strength is far greater than the sum of its individual parts.

Our edifice has been made possible by the air we press over the barrier of our teeth and roll with our tongue and lips. Sounds, which we subsequently captured in signs, have been our building stones, as the grains of sand have been those of the termites. Our cathedrals and pyramids, our articles of faith and our science, all that we speak of as civilization and culture has been built up with language – which is as literally specific to man as nest-building is to the termite.

The brain – thought – language became the biologically vulnerable human being's means of survival, as the sand fortification was the termite's means of surviving both drought and deluge. The brain begat the thought, the thought shaped the language, language organized thought, and the thinking in its turn perhaps helped further to develop the brain. The scarcely noticeable irritability of the amoeba, the elusive attentive capacity of a plant, the simple ganglia of a flatworm or a termite have evolved in man to become several thousand million co-operating brain and sensory cells. A terrestrial dust, baked together by the gravitational forces which operate between the stars, is transformed in man into thoughts which cast their own nets and capture galaxies. Carbon which cannot see, hydrogen which cannot hear, oxygen which cannot think have entered in man a union through which the cosmos can observe itself and ponder its own nature.

Life is a scale of different magnitudes. There seems to be a tendency in all matter to organize itself into larger units. Properties that we do not know form what we call elementary particles; these group themselves into atoms, the atoms into molecules, the molecules into organelles; the organelles build a cell that is an entire world in itself, so integrated that it is not only a body but a personality in which thousands of different processes take place simultaneously. Specialized cells build different organs, and combine in complex organisms; a body is a teamwork of cell masses, a complex of billions that has become one – thousands of billions of cells make a man what he thinks he is. Organisms with different biological tasks combine in the same way into what both the mind and the space camera can see as the larger organism that is the earth.

And the role of man in this great terrestrial organism? Perhaps to be Gaia's brain, central nervous system and consciousness. By comparison with the rest of Creation, we have been specialized to receive messages and information, to process them and to interpret their structures and import. Where our biological senses do not suffice, we have created artificial senses which allow us to listen to the sound of remote worlds, to feel our way through the earth and to the bottom of the sea, to penetrate matter, to capture the fields of radiation around our own bodies. Our instruments have given us a new understanding of the whole – confirming our intuition.

Man as the brain and nerves of the earth – does the analogy hold? Reality can never be entirely captured by analogies. What we find is that man needs Gaia. We have no evidence that Gaia needs man. The human brain may prove as much of a self-destructive overspecialization as the armoured bodies of the dinosaurs.

One would like even so to believe that our recklessness in relation to the rest of the earth's body – a recklessness that has brought that body close to the crisis of a fever, on the cosmic scale — stems from the fact that the awareness man has so recently evolved has not yet developed to a stage at which it can properly fulfil its function.

We overestimated the intellect. We were not aware of its potential for error. That potential, perhaps, we are now beginning to realize. As a result, a new phase of development may be opening up. For awareness. For man. For the organism that is earth.

6

Old voices whisper from the grass – the grass that gave us our existence and will one day cover us, when only the wind plays through the rusty steel constructions of empty high-rise skeletons, the fossils of our labours.

I hear the voices, but can interpret their language only in parts.

Yet they are inside me. Even unknowingly, when I speak in their accents. When I cannot interpret their language, I have failed to reach something in myself.

When darkness falls, the voices of the grass grow clearer. At the same time, space becomes deeper. The hours of darkness often afford a clearer vision than those of daylight.

On this high plain not far from the edge of the desert, the clusters of stars can delineate themselves with incredible clarity: some of them older than the earth, others younger. There hang the Pleiades, which began to condense from a cloud of gas at the time the primate line divided, and a branch with the potential of what would be the human race began to develop in the forests of Gondwanaland. There Berenice's Hair, whose tresses were combed while a fringe-finned fish crawled up from the pools on the shore of a terrestrial continent. In the clarity of night, one feels one can pass through the glittering lattice-work far out into infinity.

But here, too, I am confronted by these barriers inside myself.

In all our seeking, whether we grope our way back to our terrestrial or to our cosmic origins, we are seeking ultimately ourselves – something that can explain and give meaning to a fleeting "I" – existence.

Our agony is the narrow limits of our vision: our adventure is that we can extend those limits.

Even in the terrestrial and close-in-time, our perspectives are narrow. Our search had jerked the past closer. This has brought us a little closer to ourselves. What confines the perspective, even so, is the narrow and fragmentary nature of our knowledge, and our propensity to see the past with contemporary eyes, a propensity which basically makes all history contemporary history.

How much more narrow is not the crack in time that opens when we lift our eyes from the earth to which our bodies are bound!

The myths and assumptions in which man from time to time embodied what he thought he observed through that narrow crack were conditioned by the specific premisses of each age. They had to be abandoned *en route* as the search moved on. The deity ruling the animal-headed gods of the Nile; the god the Western world borrowed from an Eastern shepherd people, transformed for its own purposes, and then tried to make darker-skinned peoples bow down to; Ngai and Ruwa – all these were tied to a specific period in time. Similarly bound in time were the invariables in any static picture of the world: the flat earth was made round, the mechanical universe of Newton was bent, the indivisible atom was split.

Our generation has experienced a greater widening of our perspective than ever before in man's history. The pathfinders of science are advancing on a broad front. Just as the search for man's forefathers is no longer an occupation exclusively for palaeontologists, but a cross-disciplinary exercise, so too the astronomers are being accompanied out into space by a succession of new researchers – astrophysicists, astrochemists and astrobiologists. A new picture of the world is being drawn by people's collective efforts.

The results are apparently contradictory. The cosmos has at the same time drawn closer and skipped further away – closer because we are beginning to be aware how strongly the space around us is active also inside us, further away because space is widening out over an infinity that our spatially bound thought can hardly comprehend.

We have acquired a considerable knowledge about the externals of nature, which was not available to previous generations. We know, reliably, how water performs its cycle, how topsoil is formed and dispersed; we can compute with great precision the paces at which atoms divide, and the courses of planets. We do not know the structure of being, but our theories about that structure make it possible for us to imitate the processes of the sun, and the foreplay to what we call life.

With each new discovery, however, which erases a previous picture of the world, new uncertainties and ambiguities emerge. Knowing as we do how previous explanations of the world have been kindled and extinguished, we must constantly doubt the final validity of our own explanations. Far more than previous generations, we have become aware that the models of being that we make are artefacts which we must be prepared to consign to the sediment of layers of fossilized thought as the range of our thoughts and instruments is expanded.

Tomorrow's assumptions can be as remote from our own as ours are from the days when it was heresy to question whether the earth was the centre of all things.

What is new is our awareness of both the limitations of our knowledge and its uncertainty. Perhaps the greatest knowledge we have acquired is that we know so little. Perhaps the most reliable insight we have gained is our insight into the un-reliability of our observations and conclusions.

However much we extend, by our own standards, the

frontiers of our knowledge, our picture of the cosmos can never be other than fragmentary. Human observations must, as Arnold Toynbee has put it, take their bearings from the point in space and the moment in time at which we find ourselves. We shall never be able to observe other than what is closest to us in a space that is endless and in time which is bottomless. Nor can we escape from our biological premises. What we see through our crack facing the universe can be something purely peripheral in the cosmic context. The biological development on certain celestial bodies that has made possible our own observations and thoughts may be but froth on a giant wave of cosmic development.

In spite of all the things that elude the eager grasp of our thought we are entitled to believe that we have come upon what might constitute the fundamental principles of being: evolution and affinity.

Systems of thought may decay, assumptions change like passing clouds, our picture of the universe may always remain fragmentary and conditioned by the limitations of our senses – but what our intuition has perceived, our thought seemingly captured and our instruments confirmed of a constant movement, and the union of all things in that movement, points to something that we must regard as central to being.

The shuttle weaving the dynamic pattern is evolution.

Evolution is an incessant creation with components that have always existed and always will exist. Through evolution, eternal being is constantly testing new structures.

Evolution is more events than things. It is process, flow, a course of events. Things in their concrete embodiment are perishable. It is the process, the flow, the course of events that is reality. Things exist only as flow.

The immutability of evolution is the mutability itself. Individuals and species are the infinite process made finite in every manifestation of life. Being is eternal becoming.

Evolution makes everything participant in everything. Man, like everything else, exists only as a manifestation of the great flow. The only special status to which man can pretend is that he has become aware, on this splintered fragment in space, that he enjoys no special status.

Evolution and affinity are two manifestations of the same reality. The embodiments of this affinity can vary – from galaxies to microbes, from cosmic radiation to conscious creatures – but the affinity as such follows from the permanence of evolution. The affinity spans the infinities of time and space.

Time. Space. From the first dawn of his self-awareness man has tried to capture the invisible phenomenon we call time. A concrete concept of time is an experience. It presupposes someone experiencing it. Our concrete concepts of time are tied to the temporary phenomenon in time that is our earth. The measures of time that a Stone Age creature started to fixate with notches in a piece of bone afford a practical accounting system with which to register the rhythm that is the earth's and has been stamped into all earthly life. The last revolution of the earth was our yesterday, the next will be our tomorrow.

Our concepts of time give us history, and our future. They serve us in relation to the finites in which the infinite movement manifests itself. They enable us to penetrate the microworlds of the atoms, and travel over the light-years. What we capture, however, with our senses is but one of many possible life experiences even on this planet. Within the rhythm of the earth, each species has its scale and its experiential framework – the impala has its, the termite its, and you have yours.

And in the overwhelming infinity of the universe, where particles can move forwards and backwards in relation to our time scales, our earthbound concepts of time become illusory. In the universe there can be no absolute time and no absolute distances – only movement at different speeds in the relationship between different physical objects. Eternity is a quality that cannot be measured. It is there, it *is* while an endless stream of galaxies whirl by. *Sub specie aeternitatis*, time may be an extended now containing the constantly creative movement.

To modern stargazers space and time appear as two sides of the same dimension – what physicists call space-time. Space and time can only exist through the matter that is movement and affinity. One of the cornerstones of Einstein's theory was the thesis that if the universe were bereft of its matter, space and time would cease. Eternity and infinity are functions of the properties we call matter.

And so our stumbling attempts to reach ever higher in order to extend our horizons have brought us to a shelf from which we believe we can distinguish evolution-affinity and space-time as necessary conditions for each other. This has given us entirely different possibilities of experience than the static picture of the world.

What awaits us behind the crest of the next hill?

We must, after all, move on. The tangled ambiguities into which research has led us this last generation are a bush country through which we must press to obtain a better overview.

We have sought, in our research, a greater knowledge of the elements of which a whole is composed. The more we have increased our knowledge, the more our mass of knowledge has been atomized. But more essential than a knowledge of the elements *per se*, however valuable this may be, is the experience of how the different elements are related. We must now look for the whole itself, start seeking a cosmic synthesis.

The certainty we have reached of evolution as an eternal becoming, and of the affinity of all things in that becoming, may well provide a strong guiding light in the continued search.

Onwards, inquisitively onwards. The New Physics is now trying to reach a formula that can trace what we have regarded as different ur-forces, the weak and strong forces of the atoms, the electromagnetic forces, and ultimately also those of gravitation, back to a single fundamental force. The different phenomena of a galaxy, its movements in space, its burgeoning and dissolution, its dynamic chemistry and forms of life, all these could then be interpreted as manifestations of a uniform force. In this vision, the life-field of the individual organism becomes part of this uniform cosmic field of force.

Words, hewn for entirely different purposes, can hardly capture what one here seems mistily to glimpse – as little as words reach down to the domains of silence within oneself, and the processes continuously taking place there. Perhaps one can try to talk of the uniform force we are seeking as something which gives form and creates patterns. In all systems, physical and biological alike, we can trace a pattern. A cell is a complicated pattern of dependencies. The organism built by the cells is a coming and going of parts, but the whole time there is something holding the structure together. There is not a molecule in your face today that was there six months ago, but the new molecules have ordered themselves to the same pattern as their predecessors. It seems as if the individual's life-field monitors the retention of the pattern – a pattern that was inbuilt in the first fructified cell, presaged in the ur-cell – and must have existed as a possibility in an immeasurable cosmic past.

The insight we seek is an insight into *how* the patterns we recognize from our earthly existence are incorporated in the greater pattern of the universe.

Physics is concerned only with what we comprehend as physical forces. But one question asserts itself, demanding to be tested. Is there anywhere in a uniform field of force also a formula that unites what we call spirit with what we call matter?

Early man recognized early on how physical forces could influence mental, and mental forces physical – in that insight lay the power of the shaman. Now a new science, psychophysiology, is emerging from recent discoveries of the unity of living things. It may teach us to control by our willpower, our bloodpressure and pulse rate, and enable an ageing brain, whose alpha waves have subsided, to re-achieve the faster surges of youth.

The insight of the shaman and the experiments of psycho-physiology may provide a pointer, however uncertain, as we continue our pilgrimage over the blue wastes. Somewhere beyond the Pleiades and Berenice's Hair a fundamental explanation may lie waiting for us, something that will cause what we call spiritual forces and what in our verbal ineptitude we term elementary particles to emerge as manifestations of the same force.

An awareness, pondering and observing, exists only in a fast-vanishing fragment of time, which is eternities, and space, which is infinities. Everything suggests that the consciousness to which the "I" is tied is erased when the life-field dissolves. But in all its fleetingness, awareness may be one of the forms in which the pattern-creating force embodies itself. Just as in the stuff that was swept together to form a solar system and will whirl on when the solar system one day erupts, there seems to be a tendency to build ever larger structures, so too there may be also a tendency to awareness. An awareness cannot exist outside space-time. One is thus led to believe that it is an out-flow of the same force as builds galaxies.

An awareness that could not explain the elements from which it had proceeded groped its way forward by speculations about the transmigration of souls, and eternal life. In a revised picture of the world there is no room for such speculations. On the other hand, the dematerialization of matter that has started in nuclear physics and astrophysics may demolish one of the thought-barriers that previously distinguished between spirit and matter, and help to open up new paths for the continued search.

The form of awareness we feel is surely but the perceptible part of an interplay of forces uniting us obscurely with every-thing in the cosmos. It need not be the only form of awareness built by the possibilities in the cosmic pattern. Perhaps not even a particularly important one.

We must come to terms with the fact that we will never arrive at the ultimate force, the motor behind it all. As little as the termite will ever get to know the earth with whose gravel it builds its castle, can we demand finally to know why we exist, why anything need exist,

In relation to the great pattern, we are like the weaver working on his detail at the back of a great tapestry, the front of which he will never see. This means that we will never wholly arrive at the fundament of our own being.

And yet we are bound continuously to be seized by the temptation to set off beyond the horizon which our observations and accepted beliefs have reached at any given moment, to explore the explorable. Much of what now clouds our vision will be dispersed as our thoughts evolve and our instruments are refined.

The day the species stopped its search, its hour would have come, even if no hydrogen bomb threatened the earth with sterilization and no poisonous clouds hid the sun.

I hear the voices whispering in the grass. Earthly voices, but also the echoes of something from the blue savannah of space. I shall never be able wholly to interpret them, but my desire must be to learn at least something more of their language.

7

Living and dying are two aspects of the same process. Without life no death, without death no life.

Sometimes when I have sat staring into the camp-fire, the image has occurred of life as something that arose by auto-ignition in the matter of the globe, as once was the case with fire. Individual flames constantly flare up and die, but fire itself lives on through the ages, warming and combusting.

At the molecular level there is no gap between living and dead matter. Life is ignited when the matter – the properties we call matter – starts to organize itself in a certain way. Life is pattern – but only as part of a greater pattern.

Death is a redistribution of the stuff that builds life.

Death is there even when life is ignited. The death of the individual starts in his mother's womb. In its moist darkness, the foetus repeats the entire process of evolution from the primaeval sea onwards, with the fish's gills, the reptiles' gall, and the tail and hairiness of the mammal as souvenirs of its biological development. As the foetus seeks its human form, these relinquished forms disappear. Cells are born and cells die in the very first phase of individual growth.

Death, our companion even before we are born, accompanies us throughout the days of our life. Daily we die a little, daily we are reborn a little. Every day the human body rejects from itself over five hundred million cells. Every day, as many new cells are added. Life, which emerged from what we regard as lifeless, survives only by a continuous piecemeal death. Parts of the organism must constantly die for the organism to live.

The tempo at which cells are exchanged varies from one organ to another. The cells of the epidermis are so horny as to constitute, in their way, an armour plating of death. Without the protection of this armour, the living cells of the blood could not transport oxygen to the brain and muscles.

The actual cell division, the form by which even the earliest manifestations of life secured life's continuance, also changes pace. As life's day advances, the rate of division becomes slower, halting altogether in man sometime after the fiftieth division. The pattern of every species contains a biological instruction which says when it is time to shut up shop: in man, the biological potential would permit a life span of just over a hundred years, if we were not as vulnerable as we are in an environment that we ourselves have made ever more of a threat. If one freezes an organism at a certain stage, the cells continue when thawed to divide until the organism's time is up. If one places human cells in a suitable solution, they can continue to divide even when the individual's clock has stopped ticking – but they will then disown the species, and can multiply many times over the chromosomes that lend the species its genetic characteristics, becoming a grotesque biomass, a cancerous growth.

Just as the death of cells in the organism is a necessary condition for the life of the individual, so the decay of individuals and species is a necessary condition for the constant creation of life. The rhythms of decay and creation must harmonize. All life on earth dies at the same rate as new life appears, every morning, every year. The day a species could give itself eternal life, life itself would die.

In all life is the seed of death, in all death lies a preparation for new life. For a conscious creature, death is a cessation of presence. In the great flow of life and death there is no beginning, and no end.

Dust thou art, to dust returnest.

So man, at an early stage, summed up his insight that the earth was his necessary condition and fate. That he had borrowed his life from the soil, and like the grass would pay back his loan.

Given the realization that the soil, after a guest performance as life, would again become soil, it might seem a contradiction to conceive at the same time a resurrection on the last day. The traditional conceptual world of Christianity made this contradiction a dogma – and dogma is the death of thought.

But the undogmatic concept was groping in a way towards something that has been confirmed by latter-day cosmology. Particles from space and the radiation in which matter takes form when it is hurled forward at the speed of light became earthly soil and earthly life and earthly awareness. Some time in billions of years, on the solar system's last day, all this will return to space as particles and waves of light to become part of new, as yet unborn worlds. Our life flashes into being in a swell that is surging from firmament to firmament.

The new cosmology has altered nothing of the ancient wisdom, although it has amended its dimensions: from light are thou come, to light returnest.

In our own remnant of space, a surface fragment on a raft drifting over the glowing interior of a planet at the edge of a galaxy. . . . In space, at large, a manifestation of a line of evolution that may exist only on the periphery of cosmic reality. . . . A temporary and soon dissolved encounter between sun and soil. . . . Even so!

Even so, you must be filled by what is for you the enormous grandeur of the fact that cosmic matter has in you, a human being, temporarily entered a union through which the cosmos can try to investigate its own being. That you have become the bearer of an awareness which during its fleeting existence can return to its cosmic home to observe, seek, hunt its own explanation, returning billions of years before the stuff that found its outflow in this awareness will return to the blue wastes in the gaseous cloud, from something that has been a life-bearing celestial body.

Is it possible to feel this without being pervaded by humble joy at having shone for an instant in the vastness, as a breath of the organism that is earth?

The difficult adjustment is constantly to try to penetrate deeper into the mystery of life, without abandoning oneself to brooding to the extent that one forgets to live.

This, perhaps, is the art of life: continually to feel that each new day is the first day of what life remains, and therefore to fill each instant with content – with tenderness, with the joy of discovery, with empathy.

Constantly to see everything with new eyes – as if the first day of life's residue really were a new day.

8

The wasteland in which we find ourselves, this wasteland of abandoned convictions, destroyed tribal gods and decaying truths is perhaps an inevitable stage of our journey, something we must get through in order to advance.

The emptiness that occurs when deeply cherished beliefs must be abandoned can be a creative emptiness. An experiential vacuum also implies an experiential need. Now that we can no longer reach confidently for what previously lent support, our souls may have acquired a new openness for new visions.

Chaos may prove the cradle of new worlds.

Even in what is earthly and immediate. The planetary crisis that is pressing us to the edge of paralysis has not created itself. It is the work of gamblers who have put the life-bearing elements at risk. For many years they had their excuse. They acted according to the unreflecting dogma that had been jointly forged by theology and technology, to the effect that man stood outside the rest of creation and could freely exploit the planet's resources for his purposes, compressed in a white minority to a tribe's dogma of its own superiority.

This dogma too has been shattered. Even if we continue to act recklessly owing to the law of inertia that governs collective behaviour, we do so with a steadily growing sense of guilt. We are aware of the consequences of the species having stepped out of context. This is the positive thing the crisis has achieved.

Our spiritual vacuum and our material crisis are intimately related. They have both struck us in a phase of evolution at which we have turned round and seen our mistakes. The one problem cannot be solved independently of the other.

The joint crisis in our beliefs and actions is perhaps ultimately something we should be grateful for. It makes us feel the need for radical changes in our systems of thought and patterns of action. We are standing, possibly, in the as yet murky dawn of a new era, which may differ as much from our life today as that differs from the world of the early man with the catalogue number 1470, and involving at the same time a reconcilement with the origins man has for a time denied.

The great turnabouts in history have occurred when new observations and ideas have changed people's view of life. It happened when the earth, from having been the epicentre of the cosmos, was hurled out into its orbit round the sun. It happened when the message of evolution gave us a past stretching right back to the primaeval ocean.

Previously it could take generations before a new idea penetrated: old concepts defended their bastions against heresy with unbending stubbornness. The new smallness of the globe, the new means of communication, the ever faster pulse of research, and people's deep need for something on which to nail their own existence may mean that a new view of life will break through more quickly and penetrate more deeply than any previous revolution in thought.

The shaping of new messages will be the business of new generations. One, however, who belongs to a generation that has failed in much but brought some things to light finds it difficult to believe that the nucleus of the new vision can be other than a deep feeling of affinity – affinity of our own species with the earth, with the cosmos, the known and the unknown.

There is a rustling in the tree-top – or perhaps in myself. Certain questions of conscience assert themselves. Affinity?

Can I honestly feel any affinity with the Pleiades, which for yet another night will taunt with their treacherous promises of rain to a thirsting countryside? With the weaver-birds in the branches above my head? With earth, water, grass? Affinity – not just theoretically but in every fibre of my own being? The fellowship of the closed world of the clan, in which all were related to each other, was based on something tangible. But when 4,000 million have become my neighbours, how many can I experience as my neighbour? Am I not asking the impossible of myself? Is not the idea of an affinity that embraces not only the nearest but also the furthest a form of escapism?

These questions trouble me, as they are bound to. But to answer the last question in the affirmative would be to deny the possibility not only of a radical change of course but also of continued evolution. It would mean that we passively decided that the human brain *here and now*, after millions of years of preparation, has exhausted its possibilities. A capitulation to ourselves, leaving us simply to await with folded arms the bang, the big one, the last one, man's own. This, if anything, would be to flee from reality. The revolution in thought for which you are groping must be a flight back to reality.

Something in this valley carries you half-way towards a sort of certainty. When you can follow with your eyes and fingertips the course of evolution in the grey-white fossils of earlier hominids, it seems so desperately unreasonable that man's evolution should now have terminated.

Behind the contrasts, the dividedness and uncertainty of Africa today, one senses something of a restrained power. It stems from the lingering proximity to an origin.

To travel in this landscape is to brush, constantly, against something which feels essential. Africa reminds one of the context. Time and again one is struck by how people living close to nature have arrived intuitively at insights to which we are being brought close by contemporary science.

The sense of participation in something greater than self was the essence of the belief in simple societies that everything in nature has a soul. The sense of participation reflected in animism ran subsequently as a sometimes hidden undercurrent through the great religions, even when they raised towers to gods that men still could not reach because they were the creation of man himself. Religion, in Julian Huxley's definition, is essentially the reaction of the personality as a whole to its experience of the universe as a whole.

The experience need not be any the less because the god myth has to be abandoned. What science is now evoking for us is the picture of a universe in which all is united in the all. Even if we never recover the freshness of early man's experiences of life as we glimpse them behind the earliest myths and in the living fossils of our species, we should, in a new dimension, be able to obtain an experience of this universe as a whole, not as detached observers but in the overwhelming sense of participation. Does the vision not soar further that has been liberated from the fetters of the mythologies?

It should be possible, beneath new horizons, to re-unite feeling and knowing. Just as people's experience, in simple societies, of their affinity with their surroundings was combined with a sober, useful and detailed knowledge, so it is our new knowledge, however uncertain, that provides the material of which an overall experience can be forged. But the actual forging presupposes a quality beyond knowledge pure and simple. A reason that has realized its limitations must obtain help from the memories and senses of the unconscious – senses that are perhaps the instruments on which the cosmos plays.

The total experience of early man was bound to a limited sector – to us is opened an infinity. It occurs to the observer beneath one of the earth's trees that it is precisely through the experience of vastness that we can be reunited with our speck of dust in infinity. Our early explorers enlarged the earth, our new explorers have caused it to shrink. But what our space-craft, with or without human soft parts, reveal to us, what is being etched on our retinas and in our cortexes, is not just the incredible smallness of the earth in an incredible space, but also its delicate beauty.

Primitive man's stark experience of space, the patch of earth that was the basis of his material and spiritual existence, could it not, in a generation that is groping in space, be evolved to an experience of the world as a whole, without joins and seams? The early, intuitive insight that man must live in harmony with his surroundings, could it not be widened to a care and tenderness embracing our entire Tellurian environment?

Just as primitive man saw trees and springs as something to which you could listen and speak, so we are beginning to obtain a picture of the world as a single organism. We begin to glimpse the role of the species within the organism. The dogma of our superiority has been shattered. But in a way that we have surely not sought, we have become by virtue of our developed brain responsible for the further evolution of both the organism that is earth and of ourselves. We have become more involved in the earth's life than we imagined in our previous, unreflecting dreams of mastery – the brain and consciousness of Gaia.

This insight is something new we have been given. It involves a tremendous challenge.

Such a role exhorts us to humility. The wisdom of our objectives is determined not by ourselves but by nature as a whole. We must use our most refined instruments in the same way as primitive man used his senses, to listen, perceive, learn.

Immediately, the growth myth is dispelled. It is an elementary truth that we cannot, on a finite globe, go on using our resources as if they were infinite. Every organism, tree or animal, has in its life pattern an optimum for its organic growth. Man grows physically until he is rising twenty – continued growth thereafter would be grotesque, and partly continued growth would be a cancer.

Much the same applies to the organism earth. For the sake of survival, and with insight into our responsibility for continued evolution, we have to adapt ourselves to this limitation as regards both our claims on the earth's resources and the species' own growth. Such demands for adjustment direct themselves primarily at the affluent countries.

The world without joins and seams must include the living manifoldness of the human race. Consideration for the earth will be impossible without loyalty and a sense of a common fate within the species. Scanty resources render the question of distribution acute. Overconsumption in one place means reduced resources for others – now and in the future. When everyone is crowding round the same dish, one man's greed is another's death sentence. Conversely, one cannot expect any very strong sense of common responsibility on the part of those who are elbowed out.

When goods began to follow man – as the nomad had followed his food – an era commenced in which a part of humanity, by the authority of its technology, the sword, and capital, could take the lion's share of the world's resources: through trade, conquest, colonialism. That era is coming to an end.

We have reached a stage at which the neighbourly morality of the kraal should be extended to the global scale. On our shrunken globe there are no longer any ''theres'', but only a single ''here''. In the vast savannah of space, among the groves of clustered stars, the earth is a single kraal.

Can it be escapism to imagine that we who send scouts out beyond Jupiter should also be able to create a global order that ensures every creature on this fragment of space sufficient food, a daily quantum of clean water, clean air with which to flush his lungs, and a living plot of land space that is not just something temporarily left over?

The issue is the distribution of resources: in space – and also in time. There is something deeply degrading in a generation favouring itself at the expense of the future. Our responsibility to future generations is not to give them life, but to give them a world in which beauty, variety and the material prerequisites for a decent life have been preserved. Just as the clan, which stewarded a piece of land under its convention with the earth spirit, saw itself as a community many members of which were dead, some alive, and the majority unborn, so must the vision of man as the tool of continued evolution include an empathy in humanity as it extends over time.

The promises and warnings of history lie in the fact that everything that happened in the past finds expression in the present. In the same way, the future will be a product of our insights and mistakes, our visions and evasions.

In their organic context, the questions of resources and distribution indicate another way of life. Our productive and social systems cannot be left unassailed. The industrial society, as it grew from the voyages of discovery and technical innovations, has filled and overfilled its mission: so, too, has the nation state that was one of the products of the Industrial Revolution.

The industrial society has afforded great profit and liberation for certain parts of humanity which previously lived in toil and want. But as development continued, growth itself came to be the oil in the machinery and production more production for its own sake than a means of meeting people's experienced needs – with constantly greater demands on the world's resources at one end, growing mountains of waste and environmental homicide at the other. The rhythm of the machines was a different rhythm from that of nature.

The belief in progress which accompanied the breakthrough of industrialism has been followed by doubt and disillusion. Many young people have turned their backs on the industrial culture, in which increasingly few people believe; rootlessness is increasing among people who spend half their waking lives in situations with which they cannot identify. At the same time, technological development has made our social apparatus increasingly complicated – thus withdrawing it from the great majority of people, and at the same time rendering it more vulnerable. We may be approaching an age of dissolution in which desperate groups with the help of advanced technology, perhaps with plutonium in their baggage-trains, take the power into their own hands – unless we are capable of creating new ways of living together.

Via the industrial society and a nation state that no longer corresponds to the global reality, the road must run in the direction of a global stewardship, in which the laws of ecology are the laws of society and all resources are regarded as a joint asset. In concrete terms, a managing world order must probably be based on smaller, more graspable communities than the mammoth societies we have tried to construct – measuring, as we did, progress in terms of amount, volume and size. Manageable communities – and communities not escapulated in themselves but working in creative interplay with each other.

Again, old wisdom to listen to and learn from! There is nothing on this planet that any group or generation can call its own. Not the soil, not the grass, not the trees, nothing that geological forces over the aeons have stored in the earth's crust. It is all a loan to be stewarded. Tribes that we call primitive realized this. Their relationship to the environment and their simple social organization were often based on an ethic that can be summed up in the words *share* – not *own*, and *be* – as more essential than *have*.

To be – is it not this, ultimately, to which all our research must lead: to be in order to seek, to seek in order to learn, to learn in order to act, to act in order to expand our experience of being.

Even when a man's physical growth stops, he has vast opportunities for continued spiritual and intellectual growth. It is here that the great adventure of continued evolution lies.

9

Being is journeys – the journeys of the individual, of the species, of life itself. The journey of the individual, which starts in the soft darkness of the womb. That of the species, which started in these wilds, in the loins of the earth. That of life, which proceeded from a cosmic vagina.

The fateful, three-dimensional journey is present in the fate of the individual life. Everything has left impressions, however unclear, in the flesh and on the mind.

The individual's journey is short, a drawing of breath and then the end. But the journey of the species? And of life?

Again we seem to be staring into the empty cavity of a skull, once filled by a brain that contained the possibilities of both self-destruction and self-realization. It is the choice between these possibilities that we are now pressed up against, a choice that will decide the future of the species and possibly also of life in this part of the universe. We can seek guidance in the past. But no refuge.

We can never physically return to the wilds from which the species sprang, as little as a man can return to his mother's womb. As we roam about, cultivating a sense of homecoming, we know that we can at any moment, and indeed shortly will, return to the life-form that has become our own.

And yet we cannot escape the wilds. They follow in our wake, however our ingenuity may alter our lives. They are actually physically closer in our daily lives than we usually imagine. In our centrally heated dwellings and beneath our clothing, we have retained the climate of the savannah. Pot-plants, domestic animals and caged birds recall our life there. The outdoor grill, with or without expensive appurtenances, is the attempt of civilization to reproduce the mood when the prey was roasted over the camp-fire. The heat from your open fire comes as much from the camp-fires of the past in your unconscious as from the flames themselves.

At a deeper level, somewhere in the long memory of the species, the wilds are there as an imprint, a pattern of reaction, a rhythm.

When we started to deny the wilds and betrayed their rhythm, we fell as a species into an anti-rhythm, into the state in which the different elements of life separate from each other, the state that in the individual is called neurotic.

The message of the wilds and the visions of our enquiring thought converge in this: for the sake of our own health, and for the sake of the earth, we must recover our living sense of context.

The context backwards in time, which is essential in determining our own position. The context forwards, which it is essential we should grasp in order to take our future bearings.

How sudden was the development that has made us what we are! While the termite over there in its mound has not changed for fifty million years, it is only ten or twenty million years since future man and the future chimpanzee parted company. Only a few million years ago since some genetic coincidence in this valley caused the brain of the one primate to triple in size compared with that of the other. And only a few thousand years during which our species has been able to exploit that co-incidence to affect its environment, through languages that can store knowledge, and ingenious technologies, to the extent that the environment is now affecting us in a new way. A species that has developed so dramatically should have a continued dramatic evolution ahead of it, provided it does not intentionally recklessly choke its own future.

The difficult, the overwhelming aspect of our future journey is that we can no longer let our evolution be steered by external coincidence but must steer it ourselves, intentionally.

All those practising the cure of souls agree that a challenge can trigger enormous resources in the individual, which can turn a threatening tragedy into triumph. Should not the huge challenge that lies in our new insight as to the responsibility of our species for continued evolution be capable of triggering efforts beyond anything the species has previously achieved during its precipitous journey?

There is no refuge in the past. Evolution is always forwards. But without solidarity with the past, there can be no solidarity with the future. Both perspectives are equally necessary for the real and humble experience of solidarity with life.

10

The tent-pegs are pulled out for the last time, and the camp-fire extinguished. Our vehicles are loaded for the departure.

I take a last walk over to my acacia. It afforded a pleasant shade when the day was hot. It accepted my reflections and lent me something of its ease.

Daybreak, as when the pilgrimage started. Just as indeterminate, with the same elusive configurations. Dawns that cause then and now to merge.

I was a temporary visitor to the Valley, the Valley of Man. But I knew that the Valley was no coincidence in myself. Its grasses and trees, savannahs and deserts were there as echoes within me, among vaguer echoes of echoes from the forests of Gondwanaland and the breaking of the surf against a vanished coast.

A landscape contains whole series of experiential levels. As one leaves the landscape, they can flicker past in the space of a second.

Lying supine, letting one's head and feet touch their respective horizons. Being one with the grass, the blades of which strive towards the sun while the fibrous roots grope for miles in the soil. Feeling how the manifoldness of the world just in this spot and at this time flows through the senses, known and unknown, those guessed at and those beyond conjecture. Absorbing the security of the delimitation, the down-to-earth affinity. When I touch the grass, it is grass touching grass. When I run my hand over the earth, it is earth meeting earth. This is how I wanted to approach the earth: with rough tenderness, and a touch of matter-of-fact sadness – with a feeling of mutual trust.

To rise is to let the horizons fall away and a variety of other life stream into one's field of vision, one's framework of experience. To feel the sense of participation being extended, but also how something of the immediacy fades. To extend the limits of the ''I'', but at the same time to acquire a new awareness of those limits.

To struggle up slopes and see how the horizon constantly retreats. To experience the vital beauty of the effort itself, and of the new prospects that open. To become smaller the more your field of vision expands, but at the same time to be permeated by the wonder of being part of the greater structure you believe you are discovering.

Excursions in the home of man. Excursions that together make a lifetime, a short footstep in the journey of the human race.

Constantly, this inquisitiveness as to what may lie behind the crest of the next hill – the dream of Kilimanjaro.

I never reached the Kilimanjaro of my own life's journey. My strength sufficed only part of the way. Many things that I once regarded as certain, became less clear with the years. My convictions were constantly on the move, and at times lost themselves in the mists of autumn. When I have searched, the answers have often come from unexpected quarters. The fear I felt when I saw the precipices was that of joining the ranks of the living dead, those who have finished with everything and know all the answers. To live must be to seek, test, discover and ponder – and to edge one's route with cautious maybes.

Must it not be the case for our species, which bears an awareness, that whatever gives life its meaning and excitement cannot lie in anything finished but in what is dynamic, evolving, in a process of change that contains in itself the experience of the past and the possibilities of the future?

To what end were the tidal waves of the primaeval sea conducted into our veins, the limestone melted into our skeleton, the stuff of space shaped to an awareness that allowed the cosmos to contemplate itself? We will never know – and if we did, the adventure would be at an end.

But when I so avidly hope that man will give himself a chance of survival, it is ultimately in order that those who come after will be able to reach the prospects that I and the human generation to which I belong failed to attain. This feels in a way more important for me than what I myself have been able to experience. Perhaps this desire is identical with the spark that makes life burn on, while its particular manifestations are consumed.

To know as the journey of one's own life nears its end, that one is only half-way. I have been travelling for millions of years, I have millions of years to go.

The story of man cannot be allowed to end in chaos and decline. The story that started here in 1470's valley.

I rise, let my hand linger a while against the bark of the tree, and walk down to the vehicles which stand ready for our departure.

Always breaking camp from something. Always journeying towards something. Your goal is always elsewhere.

Suggestions for Reading

For obvious reasons, a tent library is extremely limited. But underlying these evening entries in my diary are, naturally, numerous books that have provided me with facts or with other nourishment for my thoughts. To assist any reader who cares to trace any threads further, I list some of these books below.

Adamson, Joy: The Peoples of Kenya (London 1973); *Anderson, Edgar:* Plants, Man and Life (Berkeley 1971); *Arnott, Kathleen:* African Myths and Legends (Oxford 1962).

p'Bitek, Okot: Två sånger om Afrika (Stockholm 1973); *Black, John:* The Dominion of Man (Edinburgh 1970); *Boyd, Andrew & van Rensburg, Patrick:* An Atlas of African Affairs (London 1962); *Brown, Leslie:* Africa, a Natural History (London 1970); *Brown, Lester R.:* In the Human Interest (New York 1974) and By Bread Alone (New York 1974); *Burr, Harold S.:* Blueprint for Immortality (London 1972).

Calder, Nigel: The Restless Earth (New York 1973).

Dammann, Erik: Fremtiden i våre hender (Oslo 1972); *Davidson, Basil:* African Past (London 1964) and The Africans (London 1969); *Dumont, René:* False Start in Africa (London 1966).

Edberg, Rolf: On the Shred of a Cloud (Alabama, 1969). At the Foot of the Tree (Alabama, 1972), Brev till Columbus (1973) and Ett hus i kosmos (1975); *Eliade, Mircea:* Myths, Dreams and Mysteries (New York 1967).

Fage, J. D.: Africa discovers her Past (Oxford 1970); *Falkenmark, Malin & Lind, Gunnar:* Vatten åt en svältande värld (Stockholm 1975); *Fromm, Erich:* The Anatomy of Human Destructiveness (New York 1973).

Gatheru, R. Mugo: Child of two Worlds (London 1964); *Gauquelin, Michel:* The Cosmic Clocks (London 1969); *Graham, Alistair & Beard, Peter:* Eyelids of Morning (Greenwich 1973); *Gulliver, P. H.:* Tradition and Transition in East Africa (London 1969); *Gunther, John:* Inside Africa (New York 1953); *Gustafsson, Rolf:* Den svarte mannens börda (Stockholm 1972).

Higgin, Gurth: Symptoms of tomorrow (London 1973).

Inger, Robert F.: Man in the Living Environment (Madison 1972).

Jackson, John G.: Introduction to African Civilization (Syracusa N.J. 1974).

Kingdon, Jonathan: East African Mammals (London 1971); *Koestler, Arthur:* Roots of Coincidence (London 1972).

van Lawick-Goodall, Jane: In the Shadow of Man (London 1971); *Leakey, L. S. B.:* Adam's Ancestors (New York 1934) and By the Evidence (New York 1974); *Levi, Lennart & Andersson, Lars:* Population, Environment and Quality of Life (Stockholm 1974).

Marha, Karel, Musil, Jan & Taha, Hana: Electromagnetic Field and the Life Environment (San Francisco 1971); *Marshack, A.:* The Roots of Civilization (New York 1972); *Mathiessen, Peter:* The Tree where Man was born (New York 1972); *Mesarovic, Mihajlo & Petel, Edward:* Mänskligheten vid vändpunkten. Den andra Rom-rapporten om människans situation (Stockholm 1974); *Mességue, Maurice:* C'est la Nature qui a Raison (Paris 1972); *Mitchison, Naomi:* The Africans, a history (Plymouth 1970); *Moorehead, Alan:* No Room in the Ark (London 1957), The White Nile (London 1971) and The Blue Nile (London 1972).

Olsen, Bo: Afrika under två miljoner år (Lund 1971);

Onibonaje, G. O.: Africa in the Ancient World (Ibadan, Nigeria 1965).

Petersen, Jörgcn: Det nye Afrika (Köpenhamn 1960).

Rapp, Anders, Berry, Len & Temple, Paul: Studies of Soil Erosion and Sedimentation in Tanzania (Daar es Salaam and Uppsala 1972); *Ricciardi, Mirella*: Vanishing Africa (New York 1971); *Robins, Eric & Littell, Blaine*: Africa, Images and Realities (New York 1971); *Rundin, Ulf*: Perspektiv på Östafrika (Stockholm 1973); *Russel, Franklin*: Season on the Plain (New York 1974); *Rydström, Gunnar*: Tanzanier (Stockholm 1973).

Sankan, S. S.: The Massai (Nairobi 1971); *Schultness, Emil*: Africa (London 1969); *Severin, Timothy*: Vanishing Primitive Man (New York 1973) and The African Adventure (New York 1973); Studies in Famines and Foodshortages (Daar es Salaam 1973); *Swantz, Marja-Liisa*: Ritual and Symbol in a transitional Zarma Society (Lund 1971).

Thomas, Lewis: The Lives of a Cell (New York 1974); *Tomkins, Peter & Bird, Christopher*: The secret Life of Plants (New York 1973).

Watson, Lyall: Supernature (New York 1973); *Widstrand, Carl Gösta*: Afrikaresenärer (Stockholm 1965); *Willock, Colin*: Africa's Rift Valley (Amsterdam 1974).

Also various special publications, university reports, and U.N. documents.

About the Author

Rolf Edberg has served Sweden as a member of Parliament, ambassador to Norway, delegate to the United Nations, president of the Swedish Press Club, and chairman of the Environmental Committee of the Royal Swedish Academy of Sciences, among other positions. He has won numerous awards, including the Dag Hammarskjold Medal in 1978. He is the author of six books; *The Dream of Kilimanjaro* is the third to be translated into English. Mr. Edberg lives in Karlstad, Sweden.